"We live in a society of boys who sh[...] [...]er-standing of manhood is at an all-tim[...] [...]wn boys playing endless hours of video games and teenagers desensitized from a bombardment of pornographic and violent images comes *Checkpoints*. I am so grateful to Brian Mills and Nathan Wagnon for creating a forty-day journey that readjusts the trajectory of development so that a young man can capture a vision for what it means to be a man of God."

— BRENT CROWE, vice president, Student Leadership University;
author of *Chasing Elephants*

"After working with collegiate athletes for nearly twenty years, I have seen a lot of good boys but very few godly men. We live in a world that has become deficient in manhood. This book is a great resource to help young men navigate the battlefield of life and not just survive but also thrive!"

— LANCE BROWN, founder and director, WhoUWith? Ministries,
"pastor" to Vanderbilt Athletics

"Young guys need to be discipled in their faith. Having a plan to do so is a must. *Checkpoints* is that plan. Buy it. Share it with others. Use it!"

— DR. RONNIE FLOYD, senior pastor, Cross Church, Springdale, Arkansas;
author of *Our Last Great Hope*

"Let the radical call of Jesus within these pages make its claim on your life as a young man and watch a man of God emerge."

— DR. ALEX HIMAYA, founding and senior pastor, The Church at BattleCreek,
Tulsa, Oklahoma

"Brian Mills and Nathan Wagnon are men who love God and are strategic in developing young men. *Checkpoints* is an incredible resource for high school guys. If you are looking for a tool that equips young men to fight temptation and live passionately for God, this is it!"

— JEFF BORTON, pastor of students, Christ Fellowship, Miami;
coauthor of *Simple Student Ministry*

"*Checkpoints* will help a generation of teenagers and young men discover principles and practices that can lead them into a disciplined Christian life. I encourage you to place this book in the hands of your young people. Also, encourage your Bible study leaders to read it and teach it. They'll be glad they did."

— DR. JOHNNY HUNT, pastor, First Baptist Church, Woodstock, Georgia

"Every young man needs to have *Checkpoints* in his life—checkpoints that allow him to stop and honestly evaluate the direction his heart and life are pointing. This book allows a young man to take a hard look at the most important areas of his life."

—JORDAN EASLEY, teaching pastor and lead student pastor, Second Baptist Church, Houston

"You won't find a better book for young men than *Checkpoints*. I love the mixture of creativity and spirituality as Brian and Nathan take us on the journey of becoming stronger men of God. This is a must-read that is both timely and great!"

—MICHAEL HEAD, youth pastor, Second Baptist Church, Houston

"*Checkpoints* is an invaluable resource that speaks directly to the very heart and issues of young men. It is a practical, daily call for men to stand up. I love it and can't wait to use it with the guys I disciple."

—MATT LAWSON, high school pastor, First Baptist Church, Woodstock, Georgia

"There are very few books that I want to put in the hands of every young man in our student ministry, and this is one of them. It will encourage and inspire young men to trust in the Lord with all their hearts."

—KEITH HARMON, youth pastor, Cross Church, Springdale, Arkansas

"This book is refreshingly different. It shows how the gospel addresses major everyday struggles of teenagers, such as pride, the pressure to perform in order to be accepted, facing failures, and many more."

—NATHAN AKIN, discipleship pastor, Imago Dei Church, Raleigh, North Carolina

"*Checkpoints* lays out clear, actionable strategies and tactics that, when applied, transform young men into emerging leaders."

—DON ROCKWELL, author of Leadership Freak blog

Checkpoints
A Tactical Guide to Manhood

BRIAN MILLS & NATHAN WAGNON

TH1NK
TH1NK, an
Imprint of
NavPress

NAVPRESS

Discipleship Inside Out®

NavPress is the publishing ministry of The Navigators, an international Christian organization and leader in personal spiritual development. NavPress is committed to helping people grow spiritually and enjoy lives of meaning and hope through personal and group resources that are biblically rooted, culturally relevant, and highly practical.

For a free catalog go to www.NavPress.com
or call 1.800.366.7788 in the United States or 1.800.839.4769 in Canada.

To our dads, J. B. Mills and David H. Wagnon —

Thanks for showing us what it means to be a man.

CONTENTS

INTRODUCTION

There is a reason Afghanistan has long been known as the "graveyard of empires." While this description is not entirely accurate, the suggestion that armies historically have experienced difficulty here is certainly true, dating as far back as Alexander the Great, some 2,300 years ago. I have never seen a more rugged country in my life. The jagged mountains and harsh winters make it extremely difficult to maneuver, keeping conventional forces at bay while providing a safe haven for insurgents. Even the flatland in the south is difficult to traverse because of primitive methods of farming: trenching the farmland to grow grapes or flooding fields to grow wheat, hashish, or opium. Yet the mission in Afghanistan hinges on the coalition forces' ability to actually get to the people, no matter how remote, and drive the enemy out of the civilian population. In this type of conflict, the infantry is crucial to success because they are able to cross any terrain though accompanied by potentially deadly risks.

In general, the enemy's operational tempo is slower in the winter months, though the attacks are much more calculated and typically fiercer. Complex ambushes are set and executed, suicide bombers drive vehicles (typically motorcycles) into coalition patrols, and improvised explosive devices (IEDs) are placed along the road or known routes, sometimes as much as 2,000 pounds of homemade explosives with fragmentation. In October 2009, an American Buffalo vehicle supporting my own unit hit one such IED, flipping the 56,000-pound vehicle upside down and killing every soldier on board.

As the weather warms, the attacks typically become less fierce, but the enemy's operational tempo picks up significantly. Small-arms skirmishes occur almost daily, and smaller IEDs are placed in fields or abandoned compounds to target coalition foot patrols. An infantry platoon's objective may simply be to move to a village 300 meters from a combat outpost to meet with village elders and conduct human terrain analysis; however, just moving that short distance to or away from the village may cost a soldier his life.

When planning a mission, it is imperative for a commander to do two things. First, he must ensure that the hazards inherent in the mission are lessened. Because a platoon is most vulnerable to ambush when moving to and from an objective, the leader must not only analyze the terrain to avoid walking into an obvious ambush point, he must also track previous routes taken and avoid high-trafficked areas, knowing that the enemy tends to place IEDs along frequently used routes. Once he has completed terrain analysis and checked previous routes, the commander chooses the route to and from the objective that gives his platoon the best chance of success. To ensure his platoon follows the designated route, the commander implements *checkpoints* along the way, and then gives the global positioning grid for each checkpoint to his point man, the soldier at the front of the formation. These checkpoints not only point the way to the objective, they also weave through hazards in the safest way possible. Following them is essential to the success of the mission and to keeping soldiers alive.

Second, a commander must utilize every asset at his disposal to field the strongest combat power possible. These assets are called *force multipliers*. Part of the planning process is coordinating with the appropriate people to make sure the force multipliers needed are available and ready. For example, depending on where the platoon is going, pre-designated targets are set so that if the platoon is attacked, it can be supported with 120 mm mortars or a 155 mm artillery barrage. Attaching a small mortar team to the platoon is an effective force multiplier because of its ability to suppress the enemy quickly. By far the most important force multiplier, though, is air support. Air-ground integration is the most crucial asset a commander can utilize because of the aircraft's ability to see the battlefield and strike targets with enormous force and precision. Not only do aircraft provide "eyes in the sky" and lethal strike capability, they also act as deterrents to enemy operations. There were multiple occasions when we had solid intelligence that my platoon would be attacked, but the enemy refrained from hitting us because we called in the birds to fly out ahead of us or cover our back as we left the objective.

All of this may seem fairly complicated and a bit confusing, but I did this every day, day in and day out, for the duration of my time in the Heart of Darkness, the district outside of Kandahar city where the Taliban was born. After daily practicing these things, over time they seemed like second nature. What is daunting at first can end up seeming mundane. However, I had consistent reminders that what seemed mundane actually set us up for success when it really mattered. It is interesting to experience the chaos of war, when lead starts flying and things are exploding around you. It is exactly in those moments that sticking to the checkpoints and utilizing the force multipliers keeps the hazards at bay and gives you the best chance to succeed.

These principles of war also apply to our daily lives. Young men face an unprecedented number of hazards every day. The world is becoming increasingly hostile on all fronts, from rejecting absolute truth to moral indifference and a general denial of God. The road to manhood in our culture is one of "finding yourself" through experimentation and self-indulgence, a process that leaves many deeply lost or scarred, enslaved to addictions and insecurities. A very real Enemy literally sets ambushes at every turn to assault a young man on his mission toward godly maturity. It is extremely difficult to maneuver the Enemy's terrain unscathed. In fact, most teenagers have had little or no training on how to move through life with skill or how to employ the force multipliers God has provided. Consequently, what remains is a mass of teenage boys wandering aimlessly through dangerous territory, one after another becoming casualties of war. The world needs skilled warriors who courageously further the mission of Christ in a hostile culture—young men who currently fill ordinary seats of ordinary homes, schools, and churches. This study is for these brave warriors.

Over the years, Brian and I have come to the same conclusion from his experience in the trenches of student ministry and mine on the front lines of the infantry: Equipping young men for action is vital. Training is required because no one just suddenly exhibits Christlike character, maturity, and wisdom. Godliness is thousands of little decisions moving in the right direction; it is practicing what may seem mundane at times so that when the chaos of life hits, a man is able to stand his ground with confidence. It is our prayer that as young men move to each checkpoint, they will learn to identify the hazards and avoid them at all cost. But this book is not an exercise in avoidance only; we aim for each young man to implement the force multipliers discussed at each checkpoint so he will not only maneuver through life with skill but also bring focused spiritual power against the Enemy, who seeks to steal, kill, and destroy (John 10:10).

Before each combat mission I led in Afghanistan, I prepared for every conceivable variable and ensured that every force multiplier available was utilized. I then strapped on my body armor and knelt in my tent, weapon at my side, and prayed this short prayer:

Lord, give me the wisdom to know what is right,
The courage to act on it,
And accuracy in my action.
My life is in Your hands.

Lord, make it so in our lives and the lives of those who take on this exercise—for the glory of Christ and the kingdom of God.

HOW TO USE THIS BOOK

Each week we will target one of eight **checkpoints** along the path to spiritual maturity and Christian manhood. We will then identify five primary **hazards** en route to each checkpoint. These will be your personal readings during the week, one a day for five days. Each day will provide a key Scripture with which you can arm yourself in the war against our Enemy; a short breakdown of how to recognize, avoid, and overcome a hazard; and **force multipliers** to provide practical steps toward victory in that area. Pray about each force multiplier and then take any appropriate action.

Finally, each week ends with an **After-Action Review (AAR)**. Read this on your own, using day 6 to prayerfully consider the questions. Then prepare your thoughts for discussion with a small group of friends or with a father, mentor, or leader. It would be most beneficial to have someone more mature as the point person for your group. On day 7, gather a group of committed guys for prayer, discussion, and accountability, using the AAR as your guide. This time of community, being open and honest with struggles or questions and giving grace and mercy to your brothers in Christ, will exponentially maximize the impact of the truths you're learning. For many participants, this may be their first experience in authentically sharing life with other people. This is where the occasion for growth really comes into play. The study will bring up core issues in personal discipleship to Jesus, so do not miss this life-changing opportunity.

Brian and I aim to take you deep and prepare you for the spiritual battle raging all around you. This book results from years of observing teenagers and young adults. The eight subjects in this study are not meant to be an exhaustive treatment of the complexities of maturing into manhood, but in our experience they are the primary chisels that shape what type of men the next generation will be. For a young man to develop godly maturity, it is important not only to train him to think rightly about the topics covered in these pages but also to actually give him the tools to practice these things accurately. We have tried to find a healthy balance between communicating complex issues clearly and challenging the reader to think and act more critically at a young age. If young men are continually treated like boys, they will remain so far too long. Within these pages you will not find watered-down language that makes the maturing process sound less difficult than it really is. The topics discussed here are real, and they are addressed in a straightforward manner. The placement of each subject is strategic, as each one builds into the next (*identity* being the foundation).

Scripture is full of stories of men pouring their lives into one another, passing along godly instruction to the next generation of leaders. One of these leaders is the apostle Paul, who challenged the church in Ephesus with the following words: "Put on the full armor of God, so that when the day of evil comes, you may be able to stand your ground, and after you have done everything, to stand" (Ephesians 6:13). We are instructed to strap on our armor because we are in a war—not against other people but against the powers that would supplant the Lord's rightful place of preeminence in our lives. It is a spiritual war.

It is our hope that you find here a challenging, biblical tool to guide you and those around you toward maturity in Christ.

CHECKPOINT 1

IDENTITY

DAY 1

Pride goes before destruction, a haughty spirit before a fall. Better to be lowly in spirit and among the oppressed than to share plunder with the proud.

PROVERBS 16:18-19

 # HAZARD: PRIDE

When you really think about it, the course of human history has shown that the essential problem with man is unchanged. The temptation for Adam in the Garden of Eden was "you will be like God," and although most people would not admit or recognize that they view themselves as godlike or want to be their own god, almost all of us act like we are. Adam gave in to the temptation, and we still do today. This hazard has wreaked havoc for millennia, causing untold suffering and destruction in the world, from the smallest children to the greatest nations. Pride is the sin from which all other sins originate; it all results from the basic attitude that we are most worthy, we deserve it, and we are the exception. Pride is the hazard that causes men to usurp God's rightful position as king and attempt to rule in His place.

Most often, pride takes the form of competition. At the core, all humans are on a level playing field. But to gain an upper hand, we selfishly tend to jockey for position and then take pleasure in the fact that we are better looking, or faster, or smarter, or more religious, or have cooler gadgets, or drive a nice car, or you fill in the blank. The *object* of our pride is only a symptom of the real problem; the true issue is the *subject* of pride — the self.

Nothing is more telling that a man is out of sync with the Holy Spirit than pride. I don't know of any verse in Scripture, occurrence in history, or testimony in which a man truly encountered the presence of

God and did not hide his face in humility. When faced with the greatness of God, you realize how small you are. Therefore, pride is often the mark that you haven't been with God. It's ironic that sometimes pride runs deepest among religious people. It's interesting that people who should realize how fallen and depraved they are often sit in self-righteous judgment of others instead of extending a loving hand to help a brother in need. If you ever find yourself heading toward having this attitude, turn around. It's a deadly trap.

One of the most effective restrainers of pride in my personal life is a quote by C. S. Lewis: "The more we have it ourselves, the more we dislike it in others."[1] When I am sickened by another man's obvious pride, jealous of how the next guy did something better, or angered by someone's gloating, I am reminded that the source of my frustration is my own pride; the deeper my frustration, the deeper the pride. Once I realize this and employ some of the following force multipliers, my frustration is replaced with empathy and I become motivated to pray that others strangled by pride would encounter the greatness of God and live not in light of their accomplishments but in the freedom of what Christ has accomplished for them.

Ultimately, pride and all resulting sin ends in judgment — judgment of others in this life and our own judgment eternally. Following Christ frees a man from the competitive pitfalls of this life. When your identity is secure in Christ, your desire is to lift Him up, honoring His rightful place as King.

FORCE MULTIPLIERS

1. *Scripture Memorization* — This is by far the most effective tool you can employ in avoiding pride. Many people are oblivious to their own pride, not realizing that a selfish disease is slowly eating away at them. If you daily renew your mind with the exercise of

memorization, you will multiply the amount of power you bring to the fight against the Enemy (and your own prideful temptations). Be careful, though; pride is a tricky business. Don't fall into the trap of being proud that you are the guy who knows more Scripture than everyone else. Find an accountability partner you trust and memorize God's Word together. There's nothing wrong with celebrating Scripture memory with your close friends — just don't go publicizing to everyone that you can recite a passage from memory. Try starting with today's verse at the beginning of this section or any of these: Proverbs 11:2; 16:18-19; 29:23; Isaiah 2:17; 1 John 2:15-17.

2. *Prayer List* — It might be a good idea to keep an active prayer list on you. In today's smartphone world, you can keep your list in a note on your phone. Get in the habit of asking people around you how you can pray for them, and then actually pray for them and follow up. Designate a time in your day that you can devote to praying for others (a lot of times I pray in the car). It's also a good idea to follow up with those people with a phone call or message.

3. *Acts of Service* — Get involved in service projects through your church or community center and make acts of service a regular part of your life. Grab a buddy or get your small group to serve together at a soup kitchen, homeless shelter, community center, or anywhere there's a need. The more you focus on other people, the less you think about yourself.

DAY 2

God demonstrates his own love for us in this: While we were still sinners, Christ died for us.

ROMANS 5:8

HAZARD: PERFORMANCE-BASED ACCEPTANCE

Most men place far too much importance on what they do, so much so that they allow their performance to define them. I would venture to say that a vast majority of teenagers would not have a solid answer to the question "Who are you?" At best, they might have a general one, like "I'm an athlete" or "I'm a student" or "I'm a musician." What naturally follows is the really dangerous part: What quality of athlete or student or musician are you? If you score the winning touchdown, you hear the roar of the crowd; if you ace the test, the teacher brags about you; if you are a first-chair musician, you get the solo. If you consistently do these things, you are the Most Valuable Player, valedictorian, or celebrated musician. However, the converse is also true: If you drop the pass, a coach yells at you; if you fail the test, a teacher scolds you; if you play out of tune, it is glaringly obvious to everyone around you. If you consistently do these things, you are taken out of the game, fail the class, or are encouraged to drop music. This is the way life is, and it is extremely dangerous for the champion and failure alike. It is dangerous because it slowly, over time, instills in us the idea that our performance makes us acceptable to the world and acceptable to God.

This hazard is especially dangerous to me. As someone who comes from an athletic background, it was very easy for me to view God as a cosmic coach, something I did for a very long time. The result was a stranglehold on my identity. My self-worth seemed to be more and more dependent on what I was doing at the time. When I served the Lord in any way, I felt acceptable to Him, like a player receiving a high five or slap on the back for a good play. However, when I struggled with sin or fell into temptation (which I inevitably did), I was overcome with a strong sense of failure; at best, I felt that the Lord was angry at me. Sometimes I felt like He abandoned me altogether.

There are many reasons this way of thinking is flawed, but through Scripture, prayer, and community, the Lord showed me two primary factors that led to this hazard in my life. First, the amount of pressure I was placing on myself was abnormal, even unhealthy. I believed that when I sinned, I let God down and that I was somehow messing up His plan or getting in His way. Obviously, this is ludicrous, but when you are blinded by pride, these lies can seem very real. Second, I was simply not believing the gospel in this area of my life. I knew, and even taught, the truth of Scripture, but I kept the power of the gospel at arm's length.

The truth is that we are acceptable to God, both when we succeed and fail, because our value to Him is not contingent on us at all. Hebrews 4:15-16 says,

> We do not have a high priest who is unable to empathize with our weaknesses, but we have one who has been tempted in every way, just as we are — yet he did not sin. Let us then approach God's throne of grace with confidence, so that we may receive mercy and find grace to help us in our time of need. (NIV, 2011)

We are acceptable to God for one reason alone: Jesus Christ. Because He is perfectly pleasing to the Father, those who are *in* Christ through faith are acceptable to the Father. Believing that your performance has any bearing on your acceptability to God essentially denies the fact that Jesus' sacrifice on your behalf was sufficient. Do you really want to do that? Do you want to try to measure up to a higher standard than that? What could you ever add to the life, death, and resurrection of Jesus Christ to make you more acceptable to God?

None of this excuses us from obedience or pursuing excellence; actually, it encourages it. To borrow from Gary Thomas, grace "is opposed to earning, not to effort."[2] When we are faithful, the Lord is pleased that we are aligned with who He has already declared us to be through His Son. As a loving Father, He already accepts us, so when we fall short or are faithless, He is not angry *at* us but *for* us, knowing that abundant life and infinite joy await us if we only quit our rolling around in the mud. When a man realizes that his value and acceptance is secure and not related to performance, it frees him to truly be the person the Lord intended. This is called *acceptance-based performance*, and *that* is God's way.

FORCE MULTIPLIERS

1. *Scripture Memorization* — Our culture comes at you all day every day with lies that fly in the face of God's truth. There is a really good reason that Scripture tells you to "be transformed by the renewing of your mind" (Romans 12:2). You must learn to counter the lies the Enemy throws at you with truth from Scripture; the sharper you get at this, the deeper you'll cut into the lies. Commit today's verse to memory. Christ's work is sufficient. He has done everything so that you may live in His freedom.

2. *Prayer* — Regardless of the reason, many of you will be susceptible to the hazard of performance-based acceptance. You might believe that your identity is directly tied to what you do and how well you do it. If you find yourself here, stop and spend time with the Lord in prayer. Take the lie to Him and ask Him to show you the truth.

3. *Accountability* — Some will have already been hit with this hazard. It will be deeply ingrained in your psyche. Coming out of this hazard and believing the gospel will be a process that takes place over time. You need to surround yourself with other men you trust who love Christ and are not afraid to come alongside you and tell you the truth in love, especially in times when it is hard to hear.

DAY 3

We are not of those who shrink back and are destroyed, but of those who believe and are saved.

HEBREWS 10:39

HAZARD: FAILURE

During Brian's senior year of high school, he felt like a failure. He'd played basketball for many years, even playing on the freshman team as an eighth grader and on the junior varsity team his sophomore and junior years. After strong affirmation from his coach, Brian felt confident that he would start his senior year, but when the time came, he did not see any playing time. Obviously confused, he felt like a failure and wanted to quit. That is when Brian's small-group leader at church told him that his character would be defined by how he handled the situation and encouraged him not to quit. Despite not getting any playing time, Brian stayed on and was able to be a great spiritual influence on his team, helping some of his teammates come to know Christ. It would have been easy for him to quit, but he surrounded himself with an encouraging community that helped him push through feelings of failure. Brian chose to believe the truth that God was working in the midst of his storm — and He was.

What about you? Have you ever wanted to give up? When faced with discouragement, failures, and disappointments, we always have a choice. We can take the easy route and give in to the temptation to stop caring or simply quit altogether, or through the power of God we can "fail forward." In John Maxwell's book *Failing Forward*, he shared a powerful illustration from Michael Jordan, one of my all-time favorite NBA stars. Jordan made a striking statement: "I've missed more than 9,000 shots in my career. I've lost almost 300 games. Twenty-six times,

I've been trusted to take the game-winning shot and missed. I've failed over and over and over again in my life. And that is why I succeed." Maxwell said, "Mistakes and failures are to be embraced because they produce lessons, perseverance, and strength of character."[3] To "fail forward" means to learn from your mistakes and failures and use them as motivation for growth in your character and spiritual life. One thing is certain: You will make mistakes. How you respond to those mistakes is the key.

One of the most pervasive habits that feeds our sense of failure is keeping score. Obviously, keeping score in athletics or academics is necessary, but we can easily keep score in areas of life where it is not only unnecessary but also unhealthy. We tend to keep score, or measure, everything. Most of you have asked yourselves questions such as *How many times have I messed up?* or *Why can't I be more like that guy who seems to have it all together?* If you tend to keep score in life, you are probably doing the same in your walk with Christ, narrowing the gospel down to a mere scorecard. Don't do that; Christ has a better way. His sacrifice did away with scorecards and every failure, both perceived and real, so that you might rest in an identity firmly rooted in Christ (Matthew 11:28-30), not in performance or the opinions of men.

Scripture tells of numerous men who were powerfully used of God but failed in extraordinary ways. In fact, that seems to be the one common thread among them all. In his book *The Root of the Righteous*, A. W. Tozer said, "It is doubtful whether God can use a man greatly until He has hurt him deeply."[4]

If you have faced or are facing failure in your life, know that God will use you greatly if only you let Him. The following force multipliers will help you unpack today's challenge and encourage you to learn from failures and move forward in the life God intends for you.

FORCE MULTIPLIERS

1. *Scripture Memorization*—To which camp will you belong—quitters or those who trust that God is at work? In order to stand strong in Christ, your identity has to be defined by His Word. You have to trust His promises. Instead of shrinking back and being destroyed by past failures, commit to memory and live by the bold declaration of today's Scripture.

2. *Journal*—In what areas of your life do you keep score? Are you trusting in the Lord or in the things of this world? To face failures in life, you must trust the Lord (Proverbs 3:5-6). Confess to God how you feel like a failure, maybe writing out your confession. Then release it to God and claim 1 John 1:9.

3. *Seek Wisdom*—Reach out to people you can trust. Sometimes these people are older and wiser (dad or youth pastor); sometimes they are simply close friends. Whoever it is, make sure he is mature and trustworthy. If you are struggling with disappointments or failures, share with these people how you feel. Have them pray with you and encourage you where you are.

4. *Study Others*—Look at people who failed but were used by God anyway. Think about David, who was considered a man after God's own heart (1 Samuel 13:13-14; Acts 13:22) yet committed adultery and murder. Paul killed Christians and, subsequently, became one of the strongest voices in the history of Christianity. There are examples on practically every page in your Bible. They're easy to find, so go seek them out and be encouraged.

DAY 4

Get rid of all bitterness, rage and anger, brawling and slander, along with every form of malice. Be kind and compassionate to one another, forgiving each other, just as in Christ God forgave you.
EPHESIANS 4:31-32

HAZARD: RESENTMENT

Can you recall the last time you held a grudge against someone? Perhaps it was a friend who betrayed you, some guy who wronged you, a girl who dumped you, or a parent who unintentionally hurt you. Perhaps this has happened recently and feelings of regret, resentment, and injustice are fresh enough that it still stings. Maybe a new kid moved into your school district and became the most popular kid in school; maybe he took your position or started dating the girl you've had on the radar. It is easy to resent him. When you probe deep enough to the core of resentment, though, you'll find insecurity, a general lack of foundation for a healthy identity.

In today's age, we are hit almost constantly by a message from society that would supplant one's identity in Christ. Popular culture bombards us with messages that identity is tied to performance, popularity, or other people. The problem with this, other than the fact that it does not line up with God's Word, is that all of those things form a shaky foundation for identity. When one's identity is based on these things, we find ourselves tossed around by attempts to measure up to some culture-imposed standard we never seem to fully reach. We end up comparing ourselves to people around us and are consistently disappointed because there is always someone bigger, faster, stronger, better looking, or more talented. This disappointment often results in resentment toward others, the frustration of a shaky identity based on a lie.

I definitely sympathize with the difficulty here. There is nothing wrong with wanting to do things with excellence, be an important person, or belong in a significant relationship; however, many people go the way of culture and end up chasing a shadow of what is intended. Young men who are held in the grace and mercy of Christ are attempting to give up their rightful place as sons of God for a perversion of it, a shadow of the real. Adolescents will go to great lengths to be conditionally accepted by an indifferent culture, a cheap imitation of what they truly seek: unconditional acceptance by a loving God.

One of the most important ways to avoid resentment in your life is to saturate your mind and heart with truth. The Enemy is constantly looking for opportunities to slip lies into your life, many times through the messages you hear from your culture every day (1 Peter 5:8). Be careful to identify these lies in your life and counter them with the truth that you measure up in Christ, and then let go of the resentment. I challenge you today to humble yourself and lay aside your resentment. Who are you jealous of? Who has angered you recently? Is it that coach, friend, girl, parent, or someone else? The following force multipliers will help you face this battle with skill and give you the tools needed to fight.

FORCE MULTIPLIERS

1. *Scripture Memorization* — Truth is the most effective force multiplier in combating the Enemy's lies. Make sure you memorize today's Scripture, and then get in the habit of reviewing the verses with your small group or accountability partner(s).
2. *Humility* — Ask the Holy Spirit to convict you. Then list the people or circumstances you resent. You might need to forgive someone for a wrongdoing, even if that person has abused you in some way. Some of you resent someone so much that you could never imagine forgiving him or her. This might be one of the easiest things to talk

about but the hardest to resolve. Humble yourself today and allow God to work through you in the way only He can.

3. *Honesty*—Be honest about your frustration; do not keep it in. Don't be superficial with the Lord. He already knows what you are dealing with, so lay it all out there. No matter how angry or frustrated you are, give it to the Lord; He cares for you (1 Peter 5:6-7). It is also very important when something is welling up in you to share it with a group of godly men. Talk to your youth pastor, friend, dad, or someone who believes in you and can pray with you. It is best to do this with another male you trust.

4. *Stay Positive*—Quit griping. Always find the positive in the midst of negativity. A negative outlook will always pull you down, keeping you discouraged and full of resentment. If you draw out the positives in all situations, your attitude and spirit will change (Philippians 4:8).

DAY 5

Whatever you do, work at it with all your heart, as working for the Lord, not for men.

COLOSSIANS 3:23

HAZARD:
FALSE EXPECTATIONS

Probably all of us at some point have been let down. Disappointment can come in many forms, from failing to be recognized for hard work to having a relationship fall apart. We all want recognition from our parents, coaches, teachers, and friends, and when that recognition or encouragement does not come, it can leave us wounded and questioning whether or not we really matter to those around us. For many of us our frustration is not limited to people or situations but extends to our relationship with God. We may pray intently for someone to be healed only to watch an illness linger on or even lose a family member or friend. Other times, we are faithful to the Lord only to be ridiculed, leaving us wondering if the Lord notices at all. It is all too common to experience disappointment in almost every aspect of life: personal expectations, family, dating, athletics, academics.

Although acknowledging that the pain of disappointment is very real, many times we set ourselves up for that disappointment by cultivating false expectations. For most, setting up false expectations has become a habit we are not even aware of. No one is ever guaranteed recognition, whether deserved or not. Sometimes other people will get credit for something they don't deserve. The reality of life is that games are lost, relationships sometimes break up, and we lose people we love. A good way to check your expectations is to see how hurt you are when disappointment comes. If you are crushed when something, or someone, does not work out like you thought, your expectations were probably unhealthy.

We are not telling you that life should be painless. For the most part, pain is the best reminder that we love. The trouble comes when the object of your love replaces the Lord as the ultimate love in your life. When this happens, your identity becomes subject to uncertainty. Maintaining a healthy identity in Christ means keeping expectations that are biblically sound. Scripture never promises that the world will shower us with recognition; it actually promises that the world will reject us as it rejected Christ (John 15:18-20). The Lord never promised that you will succeed at everything, start for your team, win a championship, be the valedictorian, or date the girl you've had your eye on. However, the Lord does promise that whatever you go through, He will be with you (Isaiah 43:2). Keeping your expectations in line with God's Word will make Christ the priority and shield you from false expectations that may otherwise be crushing.

FORCE MULTIPLIERS

1. *Scripture Memorization*—Today we've talked about keeping biblical expectations. There's no better way of ingraining these into your thought process than by memorizing Scripture. Make sure you are memorizing the daily verses. Review this week's verses, including today's.

2. *Community*—The Lord promised to be with you, and many times His presence is experienced through other people. We will talk more about this later, but do not become isolated and rob yourself of the strength and growth you will experience in community. Be authentic with people around you and share your life with other followers of Christ.

3. *Journal*—Write down some ways you've experienced disappointment in your life. Were you okay with how things

turned out or are you still frustrated? Writing out your thought process can help you see things more clearly.

4. *Communicate*—Don't expect people to read your mind. If you have expectations about a specific situation, it is best to openly and clearly communicate them in a way that is appropriate and respectful of others. This will avoid a lot of heartache.

AFTER-ACTION REVIEW

There is a reason that identity is the first checkpoint along our route to godliness. A healthy identity is crucial for your development, which is why it often comes under attack. Assaults on your identity can cause widespread chaos and confusion that might impact every part of your life. Satan knows this, so when he met Jesus in the desert, he directed the temptation at Jesus' identity: "*If* you are the Son of God . . ." (Matthew 4:3,6, emphasis added). If the Enemy attacked the Son of God with this strategy, challenging and calling into question His identity, how do you think he will approach you?

A major factor in developing a grounded identity is the ability to identify the hazards so that you can avoid or defend them and counter-attack with truth. This is why we will continue to challenge you to memorize Scripture every day. The sharper your ability to call truth to mind, the less power these hazards have over you.

Maybe you already have some struggles in the area of identity. Some of you consistently wonder if you are acceptable—if you have any value or worth. Your identity has been wounded by circumstances beyond your control, sin in your life, or both. Instead of security and peace, feelings of worthlessness and aimless wandering may characterize your life. We know because we've been there. Allow us to share some truths from Scripture that have helped us and are easy to call to mind in a tight spot:

► The Lord said he takes great delight in you, shouting for joy over you. (Zephaniah 3:17)
► He said that you are His, prized and valued in His eyes. (Isaiah 43:1,4)

▶ He promised that if you bring Him your burdens, you will find rest. (Matthew 11:28)

▶ He promised that He will turn your valley of trouble into an opportunity for hope. (Hosea 2:15)

▶ Scripture promises that the Lord will go before you, guard you, and renew your strength. (Isaiah 40:31; 58:8)

There will be times when the very foundation of your identity will be shaken. It is precisely in those times the Enemy will come and whisper to you that the Lord's promises are empty, that you have no value or worth. When you are vulnerable to these lies, lean on the greatest force multiplier: the cross of Jesus Christ. Second Corinthians 1:20 says that every one of God's promises "are 'Yes' in Christ." Could it be true that He takes delight in you? The cross says YES! Are you really cherished by God? The cross says YES! Is the Lord really able to take this burden that has defined you for so long? YES! Will God really see you through this darkness, though there seems to be no way out? The cross of Christ is your door of hope. Not only does Jesus' sacrifice make good on the Lord's promises, it publicly shames the powers that would sabotage your identity as His child. Scripture says that Jesus "disarmed the powers and authorities [and then] made a public spectacle of them, triumphing over them by the cross" (Colossians 2:15). Ground your identity deep in the roots of Jesus Christ and you will not be shaken. Although you may encounter every hazard imaginable, you will stand your ground as a young warrior for Christ. How can we be sure? Just look at the cross.

Here are some questions to help facilitate discussion in your small group. Choose the questions from each day that apply to your group the most and discuss them as a group. We encourage you to be open and honest when answering and to give grace and mercy to those around you, as you will need the same from them.

Day 1: Pride

1. How would you define pride?
2. What are some ways we become prideful?
3. Do you hate to lose? Are you an overly competitive person? Do you compare yourself to other people?
4. What steps can you take in your personal life to get rid of pride?
5. Who can hold you accountable to those steps?

Day 2: Performance-Based Acceptance

1. What kind of pressure are you under to perform? In school? In sports? In _____?
2. What has happened in the past when you have not performed well?
3. Who does Scripture say you are (and what are the Scripture references)?
4. According to these Scriptures, on what or whom is your acceptance and identity based?
5. What freedom is found in this truth?

Day 3: Failure

1. Have you gotten in the habit of keeping score of failures in your life?
2. When you have failed at something, how did that make you feel?
3. What lessons have you learned from past mistakes or failures?
4. Going forward, what are steps you can take to learn from your mistakes?

Day 4: Resentment

1. What or whom do you resent?
2. Do you struggle with jealousy?
3. What are some practical ways to stay positive in a negative situation?
4. What effect do you think a solid identity in Christ has on resentment?

Day 5: False Expectations

1. How have you dealt with false expectations in the past, and how did they affect you? What did you do as a result?
2. What has God promised you in Scripture?
3. How do God's promises affect your personal expectations?

INTEGRITY

DAY 1

Truthful lips endure forever, but a lying tongue lasts only a moment.
PROVERBS 12:19

HAZARD:
LYING

In March 2010, an outspoken and highly decorated four-star general visited our combat outpost in the Kandahar province of Afghanistan. Our area of operation sat right in the middle of an enemy transit route and was one of the most kinetic in the whole country. This general came down to encourage the soldiers by saying that in the midst of all the fighting, we were making a difference. One of the things said in his fireside chat resonated with the men and was funny to me at first, but the more I thought about it, the more I realized that this tongue-in-cheek remark was a sobering commentary on our culture's standard for stretching the truth. "When you're my age," he said, "you'll tell stories about this, and they'll be much better than they are now. Nothing ruins a war story like an eyewitness."

Think about it. Have you ever been in a conversation where every person felt the need to one-up each other? Guys do it all the time. This can sometimes get ridiculous; the truth inevitably gets "stretched" to make the storyteller look better. Don't get me wrong, sometimes exaggeration does make a story better, or at least more entertaining. However, when we feel the need to exaggerate or stretch the truth to portray ourselves in a better light (at least better than the next man), an amusing or impressive story goes wrong. This gets to the heart of today's hazard. I doubt that many of us are compulsive liars, but it would probably be safe to say that most of us feel the need to stretch the truth or exaggerate on a regular basis to compensate for what seems to be lacking.

A lie is like a small crack in a ship: The crack may not even leak at first, but the hull is weakened and it is easier for other cracks to form. One who lies, or compulsively stretches the truth, is weakening his own ship. He finds himself telling lies or exaggerated truths to cover up the initial lie. Before he knows it, cracks have formed all over the surface of his integrity, weakening his character. Then, as a ship whose integrity has been compromised, other temptations and attacks breach the hull like water, and the man begins to sink.

There may be times when you will be tempted to falsify facts in order to cover for yourself or others. You may feel pressure from friends to lie or tell half-truths to keep them out of trouble. This pressure can be intense and feel overwhelming. That is why it is important for you to decide if you will be a man of integrity *before* you are faced with the tremendous weight of peer pressure. Once your character is cracked, it becomes easier to compromise your integrity; if you lie about little things, you will lie about something big.

God has chosen us to represent Him accurately to a lost world where wrong is right. This is why even the smallest vain stretch of the truth is to be avoided. It reveals a flaw in our wholeness, an insecure belief that what the Lord is doing in our lives is not enough. As God's representatives, we must not fabricate the truth.

Being a man of integrity does not mean you will be perfect; no one expects you to have a flawless record. The trick is to seal up the cracks in the ship when they happen. Just as the little decisions weaken your character, responding correctly to failure is what strengthens your character. There are force multipliers you can practice on a regular basis that will reveal you as a man who embraces his identity in Christ, rejects embellishment for personal gain, and stands for the truth in the face of persecution.

FORCE MULTIPLIERS

1. *Scripture Memorization*—Focus your mind on the truth of God's Word. Stand firm in His promises, and the temptation to lie will not overwhelm you. Consider the spiritual truth and practical implications of today's Scripture as you memorize it.

2. *Confess*—When you catch yourself stretching the truth or involved in an outright lie, stop yourself and confess. Time does not make a mistake any better; the best thing to do is make it right immediately. This may seem awkward, especially if you are correcting a minor exaggeration, but it will prove to others around you that your integrity is worth more to you than a little stretch of the truth. This is so countercultural that you will be set apart from your peers, allowing you to give an account for why you are different.

3. *Be Honest*—When correcting a lie, own the whole lie. It is tempting when confessing to do so in a way that lessens the blow and lets you off easy. Be completely honest about your sin; this is the only way to truly seal up the crack in your character. I'm also reminded on a regular basis that the Enemy's primary tactic is to take the truth and twist it just a little. His lies resemble the truth in many ways, but he distorts the truth and leads people astray. Food for thought: When faced with difficulty in being completely honest, ask yourself if you are representing the Lord's complete truth or the Enemy's distortion of it.

4. *Encourage*—Something you can do to keep from lying or stretching the truth for personal gain is to intentionally build up other people around you. If a friend is telling a cool story, celebrate his story with him (Romans 12:15a) instead of trying to one-up him. Not only will this encourage him but your integrity and strong sense of identity will be displayed when you don't feel the need to look better than your friend.

DAY 2

The integrity of the upright guides them, but the unfaithful are destroyed by their duplicity.

PROVERBS 11:3

HAZARD: CHEATING

Cheating has become a major issue in today's society. We see it almost everywhere, from adultery to professional athletes taking performance-enhancing drugs to students copying each other's homework and cheating on exams. It can seem so simple and can sometimes be done with little to no harm to others around you, but those little actions are the ones that add up to something big.

As an example, Nathan and his wife, Margaret, were enjoying a sushi lunch at one of their favorite Japanese restaurants when they received a check that was less than it should have been. After a quick review of the bill, they discovered that a few items had been left off, totaling around ten dollars. Instead of paying the lesser amount and walking out, they simply corrected the total with the waitress and paid the full amount. I mention this not to pat them on the back but to illustrate an act of integrity. If they had cheated the restaurant, it would have proven that their integrity was worth only about ten dollars. It would have been easy to let someone else's mistake work in their favor, but that cheapens character. If we cheat someone out of ten dollars, what makes us think we would not cheat someone out of something substantial? If you cheat in the little things, you'll cheat in the big stuff, too.

The real question you should ask yourself is *What type of man do I want to be?* You never suddenly arrive somewhere in life. If you want to be a man of godly integrity, you must make the little decisions now. You must not say one thing and do another. You cannot take shortcuts.

You cannot cheat. If you want to be a man at peace with himself, you need to be willing to work hard and pay the price for everything you accomplish.

The promise in today's Scripture is that integrity will guide you, but there is another promise: Lack of integrity will destroy you. There is a consequence for every action. Some consequences are seen on the world stage, such as athletes being stripped of championships or awards because of unethical behavior. Other consequences are seen on a smaller scale, such as receiving a failing grade for cheating. But the most significant consequence is unseen: The man who sells out must live with the fact that he traded something of immense value for chump change, and that is the most difficult of all.

On September 30, 2000, the world watched a young man from Amarillo, Texas, step onto a wrestling mat in Sydney, Australia, in hopes of achieving the pinnacle of his sport, winning the Olympic gold medal. Brandon Slay's opponent was a German named Alexander Leipold, a wily wrestler whose strongest weapon was his defense. In the match, the referee awarded Leipold three points on technicalities, enough to win the bout in regulation. As the Lord was using the reality of losing the gold-medal match to refine Brandon, he received a call informing him that Leipold tested positive for steroids and that Brandon was the new Olympic champion! A new ceremony was organized in New York City, and Brandon was awarded the gold in front of a television audience of more than six million people. Since then, Brandon has used the platform the Lord gave him to tell people about the greater gold found in a relationship with Jesus Christ (Job 22:25). Brandon worked hard, trained hard, and, unlike his opponent, did not cut any corners. Although for a short time he suffered the agony of defeat, the Lord used the situation to show the world that it is worth it to keep your integrity.[1]

Most of us have cheated at some point in our lives, maybe even recently. Some of us have cheated badly and are still paying the consequences for our action. Be encouraged; Christ is all about making everything new (Lamentations 3:22-23). If you have slipped up in this area, take advantage of these force multipliers and get back on track for restoring and maintaining your integrity.

FORCE MULTIPLIERS

1. *Scripture Memorization*—Make sure you continue to memorize the daily verse. Do not mistake discipline for legalism. Forming a habit like Scripture memorization is disciplining yourself for the purpose of godliness (1 Timothy 4:7b). If you do this consistently, what do you think will come to mind when you are tempted to cheat?

2. *Ask the Tough Questions*—How have I cheated? List the ways you are cheating and how you need to change. We have all made mistakes and have all cheated at some point, so be honest with yourself when asking this question.

3. *Work Hard*—Most of the time, cheating is the result of laziness. Cutting corners and taking shortcuts is easy to do, but it doesn't truly pay off. There is satisfaction and fulfillment in accomplishments only on the other side of hard work, so don't cheat yourself out of that.

4. *Confess*—This is a step that will take you from being a boy to becoming a man. True men of character confess and make wrongs right. Have you stolen something? I challenge you to return the item and confess. Have you cheated on a test or schoolwork? I challenge you to confess to your teacher and take the penalty. First confess to God, and then be a man and own it with those you have wronged.

5. *Move On*—Once you have confessed and made things right, receive the forgiveness of God (1 John 1:9) and press on in the race God has called you to run.

DAY 3

No matter how many promises God has made, they are "Yes"
in Christ. And so through him the "Amen" is spoken by us to the
glory of God.
2 CORINTHIANS 1:20

HAZARD:
BROKEN PROMISES

We live in an unreliable world. It is common for promises, big or small, to be neglected or broken. We consistently hear promises from almost everyone — from politicians and government officials to family and friends — that are often unfulfilled. Seldom do you find someone who truly values his word and does whatever necessary to fulfill an obligation. Our culture has progressively moved toward the belief that keeping one's word is optional as long as it is convenient or advantageous.

As humans, we bear the image of God. As His representatives, we reflect His character to the world. Scripture tells us that all of God's promises are kept in Christ (2 Corinthians 1:20), so as His representatives, it is crucial that we be men of our word. It is important to be reliable because God is reliable; it is important to keep your word because God keeps His word. It is important to accurately reflect Christ because you are who the world sees.

It is no wonder the world's view of God is insufficient or altogether wrong. Some people claim the name of Christ but sacrifice their integrity for convenience or personal gain. If the people who bear His name act no different from everyone else, what does that say about the nature of God? It is time for young Christian men to embrace their identity in Christ and the integrity that follows. We need teenagers and young adults to swim against the stream of modern culture and actually keep their word — to be a reliable person when no one is looking, not because something is to be gained but because that's how God is.

In the late summer of 1994, Nathan graduated from junior high football to the high school team. The difference between the two was immediately apparent when two-a-days started in early August. Most sophomores play for the scout team, which runs plays against the varsity players to prepare the starters for the week's opponent, an assignment no one really cares for. After days of consistently getting beat up in the miserable Arkansas heat, Nathan had had enough. Following one morning practice, he told his dad that he did not want to return for the afternoon session — that if this was football, he wanted nothing to do with it. After hearing his complaint, Nathan's dad informed him he would return and finish out his commitment to the team (even though he sat the bench almost every Friday night that season). Nathan went on to be a successful high school football player, and he looks back to that day as a formative experience when he learned the importance of being a reliable young man.

What about you? Are you reliable? Do you go back on your word when that commitment gets difficult or costs you something you weren't counting on? Do you abandon promises because something better comes up? Do you slack off when no one is looking, or do you work hard regardless of who sees you? Would the people around you say you are a man of your word?

FORCE MULTIPLIERS

1. *Scripture Memorization* — When faced with the temptation to break a commitment or go back on your word, the Scripture you put to memory will be the primary asset that keeps you grounded. It's amazing how in moments of weakness, the Lord brings certain passages to mind. Keep at it.

2. *Finish What You Start*—This may sound fairly elementary, but it is consistently practicing the basics that will distinguish you as a man of your word. Many people start something and then quit when it gets tough or demands more than they're willing to give. If you give your word to do something, see it through to completion. Jesus knew that going to the cross wasn't going to be easy—aren't you glad He finished what He started (John 19:30)?

3. *Do the Right Thing*—Even when no one is looking. Being a man of integrity means you act the same regardless of who is around. This is the true test of your integrity and the one you will probably fail the most; anyone can do the right thing when everyone is watching. The importance of accountability here cannot be overstated. Bring other trusted men into those areas of your life where you are weakest and draw strength from your community.

4. *Underpromise and Overdeliver*—There will be times when you have the purest intentions and, because of ambition or naiveté, promise something you cannot deliver. It is a good idea always to consider that unforeseen event or issue that could hinder you from fulfilling your word. Take it from guys who have been there: It is better to underpromise and overdeliver than to overpromise and not fulfill your word. Be sure that when you give your word, people can count on it.

5. *Own Your Broken Promises*—When you do break a promise or go back on an obligation, go to the person or people you offended, humble yourself, and make things right. This is the act that allows you to maintain or regain your integrity in the midst of mistakes or outright sin.

He who conceals his sins does not prosper, but whoever confesses and renounces them finds mercy.

PROVERBS 28:13

HAZARD: HYPOCRISY

A 2007 study showed that 87 percent of young non-Christians said that present-day Christians are judgmental, and 85 percent said they are hypocritical.[2] There are two extremes of hypocrisy: The pious, judgmental extreme is reflected in this Barna study; the other is much more subtle. We must deal with both to accurately reflect the nature of Christ.

There is a tendency among American Christians to go after moral and ethical issues in the public arena. More often than not, "go after" can mean an all-out assault on non-Christians who hold differing views; this is a tactic that looks nothing like Jesus' call for people to follow Him. Frankly, I've never understood why we expect lost people around us to "get it." Lost people don't understand because they're lost; we should not be surprised by their lostness. To be fair, most Christians have good intentions, but the tone outweighs the message that is then lost on deaf ears. A rift is created between mostly well-intentioned Christians and a lost world. When people get close enough to us to see that we're far from perfect and have sins much like (or even worse than) the people we're calling out, we earn the reputation of being hypocritical and judgmental. Maybe you've heard someone say something along the lines of "Who are you to point out anything in my life when you have your own problems?" Sometimes the very things Christians rage against are alive and well in their own lives.

The other, subtler form of hypocrisy is illustrated by a bumper sticker I've seen around. It reads, "Christians aren't perfect, just forgiven!"

I have known a handful of Christians who have misunderstood God's grace as a free pass to do whatever they wanted. They open the door for all kinds of blatant sin. This is a reverse hypocrisy; instead of trying to hide their imperfections, they celebrate their sin. They claim to follow Jesus but do nothing to actually follow Him.

Both instances are hypocritical, saying one thing but doing another. Both misrepresent the name of Christ we take as Christians. But wisdom is found in the middle. As for the overly pious, it is important for us to place a high value on living a righteous life, but only as a means and not the end. Devotion to God is the means by which we relate to Him (prayer, time in the Word, church); God Himself is the end. As soon as piety becomes the end, we have arrived at legalism, the condition Jesus raged against the most. Also, like the opposite extreme, we must place a high value on God's grace, but not to the point of abusing it or misunderstanding it altogether. Gary Thomas said that grace "is opposed to earning, not to effort."[3] In Christ, the old things have passed away and everything is made new (2 Corinthians 5:17). It is hypocritical of us to ignore the fact that through the Cross, God made us new.

We must live out the change God has brought about through Christ, embracing the fact that His grace is waiting to pick us up when we fail. Because of the power of the gospel, we are able to get up and keep moving toward Christlikeness, not hiding our sin or pretending it doesn't matter. We must be honest and humbly own our imperfections to lost people around us and, at the same time, live lives that strive every day to accurately reflect Jesus. This combination will dispel accusations of hypocrisy and draw attention to an authentic gospel, allowing us to give an answer for the hope we have in Christ.

The most difficult aspect of this is not knowing what to do but actually doing it and doing it with skill. There may be some embarrassing situations where you slip up in front of people and do the very thing you stand against. You may have to confess publicly and ask forgiveness for the gap between your action and your faith. Do it, and do it right then.

A man of God owns his stuff and makes it right. Here are some practical steps you can take to avoid hypocrisy.

FORCE MULTIPLIERS

1. *Scripture Memorization*—Make sure you commit today's verse to memory; it's a great reminder that healing is found in owning your mistakes and making them right.

2. *Confess and Renounce*—Confession is the first step to healing, but it is not enough to just go on confessing the same sin over and over—you must change. Too many of us say that we want to change, but in reality we have no intention of giving up our sin. The second aspect of healing is to abandon your sin. This may involve taking practical steps with your accountability partners to stay away from the things that trigger temptation or to go through an organized recovery program. Whatever it is, you must both confess and renounce your sin.

3. *Authenticity*—It can be scary to honestly put yourself out there, but don't try to be someone you aren't. You'll be surprised at the level of acceptance you receive when people realize that you aren't perfect and that in the midst of your imperfections, Christ is working inside you.

DAY 5

Trust in the LORD with all your heart and lean not on your own understanding; in all your ways acknowledge him, and he will make your paths straight.

PROVERBS 3:5-6

HAZARD: MANIPULATION

Webster's dictionary defines manipulation as "to control or play upon by artful, unfair, or insidious means especially to one's own advantage." It is one of the primary tactics used pretty much across the board, whether knowingly or unknowingly, to attempt to control situations. There is a natural inclination in all humans to push the envelope and find out how much we can get away with. This can be clearly seen in young children who rebel against parents and then play authority figures against one another in an attempt to exercise control over a situation. Although we would like to think we all grow out of this tendency, I'm afraid the problem only takes on a more serious tone as we get older.

If left unchecked, our manipulative nature will manifest itself in every area of life, sometimes even out of habit. Probably the most common area of manipulation is dating. There is a reason the beginning of relationships is often the most attractive: Neither person is being completely honest. No one in his right mind is going to delve into the ugly areas of his life with a good-looking girl he just met. On the contrary, he will probably go to great lengths to put his best foot forward, even if that foot is not actually *his* foot. This is entirely natural; however, when facts are stretched or an altogether different person is portrayed in order to win the girl over, the old habit of manipulation has just kicked in. In extreme cases, a guy will take what he has learned about a girl to pull the right strings and say the right words so she melts in his hands and he ultimately gets what he wants (most of the time it's sex).

If not already, there will be times you're faced with losing something of great value to you or gaining something you've always wanted. The temptation will be to manipulate the people around you to get, or keep, what you want. Whether it is pitting authority figures against each other (parents, coaches, bosses) or attempting to change the game through cheating or altering facts, the result is always the same: Your integrity is weakened or broken. Ultimately, we have decided that the thing we have a vice grip on is worth gaining or keeping, even if it costs us our integrity.

It is not wrong to win over a girl, gain popularity, or hold on to that thing you value; it is only wrong when you must manipulate to do so. You can achieve great things or meet honorable goals, but getting there is only half the issue; you must also accomplish these things the right way. This translates into our relationship with the Lord as well. How many times have you asked God for something and been told no or to wait? Typically, the conversation moves toward some sort of bargain. We tell God that if He gives us what we want now, we will do something for Him (as if He needs it). Sometimes our intentions are pure and convey a worthy cause, such as a family member being healed or a friend being rescued from addictions. However, we want things to be made right immediately, when the Lord's plan may involve suffering—suffering that results in our ultimate good. This type of scheming with the Lord is veiled manipulation. We want God to do things our way in our time, as though we know better than the Sovereign of the universe.

Are there areas of your life where you can see blatant manipulation? Is there something or someone you should release to the Lord? Do you find yourself making deals with God or becoming angry with Him when things don't go your way? First, you are not alone. This problem is not specific to you, so get in line. Second, there are a handful of force multipliers that will give you the tools you need to be a man who has no need for manipulation—a man who draws his strength and rest from his relationship with God.

FORCE MULTIPLIERS

1. *Scripture Memorization*—Sometimes manipulation is so subtle that it's difficult to detect. Scripture is one of the primary ways the Holy Spirit will convict you regarding areas where you need to trust the Lord. Your wisdom in these areas will increase as you commit God's Word to memory.
2. *Hold Things Loosely*—If you can get good at this, you will be wise beyond your years. Everything good in your life is from the Lord; it is His to give and His to take away. The sooner you realize that your ultimate good is found not in what He gives you but in Him alone, the looser you will hold things that aren't eternal anyway.
3. *Be Honest*—Write down the ways you manipulate others. Take some time on this. Look back at this past week and think through what you have done. The key to maturity is learning to reflect on your experiences and learn from them. How did you manipulate your parents? Your coaches? Your teammates? Your friends? Girls?
4. *Confess*—Confess your manipulation tactics to God and ask for His forgiveness right now. Just say out loud what you have done and release it to the Lord, and then share this with your accountability partners or small group.

AFTER-ACTION REVIEW

The essence of integrity is wholeness; it is a life put together. The man of integrity is not perfect, but he is secure in God's life-changing grace. He is vulnerable, authentic, and unafraid of failure, knowing that his shortcoming is an opportunity for growth. He does not need to fear being found out because he keeps short accounts and humbly owns his mistakes to those offended. The man of integrity has no need to lie or stretch the truth because he is held together by the sufficiency of Christ. He does not take shortcuts because he understands the journey is as important as the destination. He is a man of his word because he represents a God who keeps His word. The man of integrity has no need to manipulate the world around him because his trust is in the sovereign Creator and Lord of the world and everything in it.

He is a man who rejects hypocrisy, embracing his role as an ambassador in a broken world—a world that is being redeemed. His character sets him apart from everyone else around him and brings weight to his witness. His words are as skillfully chosen as the wisdom he displays living among those separated from the Almighty. As the Savior's ambassador, he calls them to an intimate relationship with their Creator, not only with his words but also with his life. He is not perfect, but he is a man of integrity, and we need more men like him.

Will you be this kind of man? Will you reject the world's idea of manhood and embrace what it truly means to be a man? Anyone can boast about himself; anyone can take shortcuts; anyone can sacrifice his integrity to vainly pursue temporary satisfaction. Christ has set you apart and given you the strength to be different. He is calling you to swim upstream in our culture, not recklessly leaving a wake of destruction behind you, but, with accuracy and skill, leading a life of integrity that shines like a city on a hill in a dark world.

Around three thousand years ago, the Lord set apart a young man to lead—a young shepherd of no reputation who became the greatest king in the history of God's people.

> He chose David his servant
>> and took him from the sheep pens;
> from tending the sheep he brought him
>> to be the shepherd of his people Jacob,
>> of Israel his inheritance.
> And David shepherded them with *integrity of heart*;
>> with *skillful hands* he led them. (Psalm 78:70-72, emphasis added)

We have no doubt the Lord is calling you to a similar life. You may not be a great king, but you serve a great King, one calling you to shepherd the people around you with integrity of heart and skillful hands. Answer the call. Do not settle for anything less. Stand firm and be a man (1 Corinthians 16:13), and then give glory to the Ultimate Man.

Here are some questions to help facilitate discussion in your small group. Choose the questions from each day that stick out the most and discuss them as a group. Remember, we encourage you to be open and honest, giving grace and mercy to those around you, as you will need the same from them.

Day 1: Lying

1. Have you ever exaggerated a story to make the story or yourself look better? Does that actually make you better or worse?
2. What lies have you told this week? Have you stretched a story, not told your parents the truth, or lied to a friend?
3. Is a small lie okay? The answer to this question can be found as you go back and read about the "crack in the ship."

Day 2: Cheating

1. How is cheating looked upon in today's culture? Where have you observed someone cheating recently?
2. How does cheating in the "small things" push you to eventually cheat in the "big things"?
3. You were asked in the lesson what type of man you want to be. How do you answer that question? What are five characteristics you would like people to see in you as a young man?

Day 3: Broken Promises

1. Have any of you ever experienced broken promises? Give an instance of when you or someone you know promised something and never came through.
2. How do you think broken promises are hurting relationships today?
3. Would you consider yourself a reliable man? How have you proven you are reliable?
4. One of the force multipliers was to underpromise and overdeliver. What does that mean, and how do you apply that to your life?

Day 4: Hypocrisy

1. What characterizes a hypocrite?
2. In what ways do you use God's grace as a license to do whatever you want?
3. What does the quote "Grace is opposed to earning, not to effort" mean?
4. What does an authentic Christian lifestyle look like?

Day 5: Manipulation

1. Have you ever manipulated someone or a situation to get what you wanted?
2. Where do you see manipulation taking place the most (dating, with parents or coaches, at work)?
3. What does holding things loosely mean to you? What does this look like in your life?

COMMUNITY

DAY 1

Have nothing to do with the fruitless deeds of darkness, but rather expose them.

EPHESIANS 5:11

HAZARD: ISOLATION

Have you ever been separated from your family and friends in the midst of a crowd? I have, and the funny thing is, I felt totally alone. I was surrounded by hundreds of people, yet I felt alone. I wonder how many of us live our lives like this; we surround ourselves with "friends," yet in our vulnerable moments, we readily admit that although we are acquainted with many, we are truly known by none. Friendship is often an exercise in keeping up appearances at all costs, covering up anything that might show weakness or flaw. We spend most of our time working to achieve the desired or expected role among a cast of characters, yet all the while, our true selves are shut up, double bolted, keys thrown away. Sound familiar?

Most people live in isolation out of fear of exposing the ugly parts of their lives: the selfishness, lust, hatred, lies, envy. We are ashamed of these aspects of our lives, yet exposing these things is the first step in overcoming them. Paul teaches in the New Testament that when left to ourselves, we will war against God's plan for our lives (Galatians 5:17). The simple fact is that isolating ourselves, or keeping certain dark closets locked, only feeds our natural rebellion against God. Some may think the shameful aspects of our lives will simply disappear if we only shut them away, but it is this very act that feeds them, causing them to fester and grow. This is why the Lord calls us to walk in the light, exposing the dark parts of our lives to trusted people around us.

Two things happen in the light. First, what is exposed is done away with (Ephesians 5:13), and, second, the fruit of the Spirit grows

(Galatians 5:22-23). Isolation feeds the flesh; the fruit of the Spirit thrives in community.

True community occurs when we step out of our comfort zones and get serious about living out in the open. This does not mean we should throw all caution to the wind and carelessly tell everyone around us our deepest, darkest secrets. It does mean that we search out trustworthy Christians, people able to give wise counsel when we uncover those hidden corners of our lives. These people should be mature and willing to listen and empathize with our struggles while challenging us to abandon our sin and run hard after the Lord. Unfortunately, this type of person can be hard to find. If you have never been in a friendship like this, ask God to bring a true friend your way and then go about *being* the type of friend to others you would want to have. It is amazing what happens when we choose to take the focus off ourselves and love people as Jesus did, with grace and truth.

Probably the harshest punishment known to man is solitary confinement. A person is taken out of any sort of social environment or community and is left to himself, totally isolated. Although there are few people who literally isolate themselves physically, a great many of us sentence ourselves to spiritual and emotional solitary confinement, totally blocked off from any real form of community. We turn inward and focus solely on the self and then slowly wither and die. C. S. Lewis described this type of person: "He has his wish — to lie wholly in the self and to make the best of what he finds there . . . and what he finds there is Hell."[1]

What are the hidden corners of your life? What are those things you are afraid to share with anyone else? Do you deliberately conceal parts of yourself because you are afraid of what others might think or do? Let it go. Reject the temptation to turn inward and focus on only yourself. Let others in. No one is asking you to be perfect, just real.

FORCE MULTIPLIERS

1. *Scripture Memorization*—There are some great verses that instruct children of God to reject isolation and live in the light; today's verse is one of them. Memorizing and applying Scripture to your life will give you the strength you need to resist the temptation to turn to isolation as well as the wisdom to be the type of friend who cultivates an atmosphere of authenticity and faithfulness. Also check out John 3:20, Galatians 5:16, and Ephesians 5:8-14.

2. *Accountability*—This is one of the most critical assets you can bring to the fight against isolation. As mentioned on pages 56–57, you must find a true friend—someone who loves Christ and is trustworthy. If there is no one, ask God to send a friend, and then *be* that person for others around you. Once you have found a true friend, follow these suggestions:

   ▶ Set a time to get together during the week, and then consistently meet to sharpen and encourage one another. Make this a high priority; consistency is key.
   ▶ During the first few times you get together, share life stories with one another. Find out about each other's families, backgrounds, strengths, struggles, defeats, and triumphs.
   ▶ Once you know each other fairly well, make a list of questions that will hold each person accountable to struggles or sin issues.
   ▶ Although it is important to focus on confession and repentance, don't dwell on sin issues all the time. If there is victory, celebrate it!

3. *Be Vulnerable*—The opposite of isolation is not just disclosure but full disclosure. Don't fall into the trap of only cracking the door open; fling the door open. Be completely honest. Leave nothing

unsaid. Let people in. But remember to be wise about to whom you vent or confide. It can be hurtful to have no filter in every situation. Find good friends (other guys), mentors, youth leaders, coaches, teachers, and parents with whom you can be completely vulnerable and brutally honest.

DAY 2

*If you are offering your gift at the altar and there remember that
your brother has something against you, leave your gift there in
front of the altar. First go and be reconciled to your brother; then
come and offer your gift.*

MATTHEW 5:23-24

HAZARD:
CONFLICT

There are few certainties in life, but one of them is that people will not
always get along. Conflict is a part of life. We should not be surprised
when disagreements among family or friends occur, or when relationships are strained. Although relationships are the greatest source of joy in
our lives, they can also bring the most pain. The closer the relationship,
the greater its capacity for either fulfillment or disappointment. Instead
of wallowing in the pain that accompanies conflict, we should embrace
these situations as unique opportunities for growth.

Typically, people will go to one of two extremes when dealing with
those who have hurt them. The first response is alienation. When we are
hurt, our natural response is to protect ourselves from ever being hurt in
the same way again. We will distance ourselves from the offending person
at all costs. In casual relationships, this might not have far-reaching
effects; however, when it is your best friend or your parents or a sibling,
the distance created by your movement away from them is a noticeable
reality. In severe cases of alienation, one may even physically run away
instead of actively dealing with the conflict. The second extreme response
is aggression. We may be so angry that we lash out, if not physically then
with our words and attitudes, seeking to inflict the same amount of
damage on the one who hurt us. This response can also include other
forms of aggression, such as dwelling on ways we can get payback,

making passive underhanded remarks, or talking behind a person's back. We don't look to separate ourselves from the person; on the contrary, we want to stay close enough to inflict damage. Neither of these responses is effective in resolving conflict, nor does it glorify God.

The answer is found somewhere in the middle. A person who views conflict as an opportunity for growth doesn't run away from it or pursue retribution. If he is hurt, he acknowledges his pain and may even spend some time alone to process what has taken place, but he does not stay there. With sincerity, he quickly moves to acknowledge and ask forgiveness for his part in the conflict and then humbly communicates the way he has been hurt. He is not seeking revenge but reconciliation. Regardless of whether the other person asks for forgiveness or not, he forgives. When I am tempted not to forgive others, the Lord quietly reminds me that I am in need of forgiveness every day. Thankfully, His mercies are new every day.

There will be times in your community when you will want to wash your hands of it all and walk away—a fight among friends, careless words spoken, blatant disregard, or even betrayal. It is what we do in these moments that makes or breaks us as a community of Christ followers. In case you are tempted to walk away, remember that Jesus thought people were worth fighting for, even those who betrayed Him and nailed Him to a cross. Jesus' sacrifice on the cross is the ultimate conflict resolution. The conflict we would not and could not resolve, He took upon Himself and redeemed (2 Corinthians 5:21). This is the example we should follow. Fight for your community; it is full of people for whom Christ died.

FORCE MULTIPLIERS

1. *Scripture Memorization*—Keep up the great work. You're establishing a life-changing routine of taking God's Word to heart. Consider the eternal truth and immediate application of today's Scripture.

2. *Think Before You Speak or Act*—One of the most practical things you can do to avoid conflict is to simply think about the consequences of your words or actions before you say or do them. Most of the time, we don't set out to create conflict with our family or friends; however, careless words or actions can cause a lot of damage. Try to put yourself in the other person's shoes and think about how that person would respond to certain words or actions. Don't over-analyze this; just make it a habit to think of others before you say or do something (Philippians 2:3-4).

3. *Keep Short Accounts*—To ensure that conflict is not allowed to fester and grow, it is imperative to address it quickly. Depending on the depth of the offense, allow a reasonable amount of time to process what was said or done. Just make sure that too much time does not pass or it will open the door for bitterness and anger to creep in and take hold, making reconciliation a much more difficult process.

4. *Communicate*—It is crucial when resolving conflict to communicate clearly. Many times, conflict gets worse because we fail to communicate or, if we do, we do so poorly. When clearing up an offense or righting a wrong, it is vital to show humility. Any aggressive stance or posturing will only make matters worse. If you were offended, make sure you are completely honest about the damage done, but do so in a tone that seeks reconciliation, not retribution.

5. *Listen*—Especially if you own a majority of the responsibility, listen to the other person with understanding, even if you disagree with what is said. You may have to sift through emotion to really hear what is intended. Listening with humility allows you to empathize with the other person's pain and accurately ask for forgiveness.

6. *Ask for Forgiveness*—Rarely does a conflict situation contain only one responsible party. Most often, both parties share the responsibility for wrong done to varying degrees. Even if you think the other person owns 90 percent of the guilt, it is still important for you to own your part of the conflict, especially before you begin to talk

about how you were offended. When you confess your stuff, confess all of it; do not leave anything undone that could continue to be a barrier. Name the wrong you've done, be specific, and then ask for forgiveness. It is not enough to say you are sorry; asking for forgiveness is what bridges the gap.

DAY 3

Without wood a fire goes out; without gossip a quarrel dies down.
PROVERBS 26:20

 **HAZARD: GOSSIP**

A male-dominated culture can sometimes be overly macho, defined by the desire to be just as, if not more, "manly" than the next guy. We discussed this on the day about "Pride" at checkpoint 1; however, one of the ways pride manifests itself is by tearing others down. Insecurity can show itself in an attempt to increase self-worth by bringing others down.

How often do you talk behind someone's back, saying things to others you would never say to that person's face? Have you recognized a need to know what is going on with everyone around you, especially if it is something scandalous? I would venture to say that a majority of us participate in these things consistently to varying degrees.

Gossip is a more socially acceptable sin that is practiced in our culture without restraint. There is even an entire entertainment industry devoted to celebrity "news." Although we may acknowledge this sin of gossip, followers of Christ engage in gossip as well. Sometimes it's under the guise of showing concern for a person or sharing a personal prayer request without permission. Sadly, it is too common for insecure Christians to take information given in confidence and spread it around just to show they are important enough to be in the know.

It is essential when building and maintaining a strong, Christ-centered community to cultivate an environment of trust. There cannot be authentic Christian community without sharing all of life—the triumphs and failures, the difficulties and victories—with trusted friends. People need to know that when they share a struggle, others will not use that information to exploit them. It can be catastrophic when a member of a community betrays confidence through gossip. This will immediately derail the community; what used to be a safe place to be open and honest has been compromised. Through one simple act, the work of God in a community of believers can be severely hindered. The importance of this cannot be overstated; if someone shares something in confidence, keep it to yourself.

A strong Christian community places a high value on dependability. These Christ followers consistently reject the temptation to spread gossip and graciously stop it when they hear it going on around them. The only thing we should be spreading around is encouragement and confidence in Christ. If we consistently participate in gossip, an environment of secrecy and betrayal will grow around us; however, if we are secure enough in Christ to refuse gossip and actively participate in building others up, an environment of safety and trust will grow around us. Just like the proverbial fire in today's verse, whatever we choose to feed grows.

Do you feed gossip or trust? You may hear gossip going on all around you; step out and be the change you seek. Choose to be a man of God and build others up instead of tearing them down. Choose to stand in the gap for the marginalized who are consistently the subject of gossip. Choose to be the example others should follow and you'll find you are growing a safe, Christ-centered community where real friendships will develop and thrive.

FORCE MULTIPLIERS

1. *Scripture Memorization*—Today's verse is a good reminder that starving gossip is like starving a fire. If you refuse to give it fuel, it will go out. Each careless word is a log thrown on the flames. Scripture memorization allows you to keep truth readily available to use at a moment's notice. It would be interesting to know how many

times this truth comes to mind when you are faced with the temptation to participate in gossip.

2. *Stop Before It Starts*—Whether you catch yourself starting to gossip or you are in a conversation where someone begins to gossip, stop it before it gains momentum. If you are the culprit, stop immediately and explain to those listening that you should not have said anything. If someone else begins to gossip, gently remind him that we should not talk behind others' backs. If that person refuses to stop, graciously excuse yourself from the conversation. This may be awkward because it is so countercultural, but you will distinguish yourself among your peers as one who is trustworthy (1 Peter 3:15).

3. *Keep a Secret*—This may seem extremely obvious, but sometimes it can be difficult to practice. However, doing so will show the people in your community that you place a high value on them and their trust in you. Doing something as simple as not telling a secret cultivates the type of environment needed for people to open up and be real, allowing real life change to occur.

   There is one exception that needs to be noted here: If the secret involves that person's endangering or harming himself or anyone else, appropriate action needs to be taken. Before you tell anyone, humbly inform your friend that others need to be brought in to provide counsel. Encourage that person to go with you to talk to someone who can help, such as a parent or trusted leader in your church. The intent is not to rat out your friend but rather to protect him and others by getting him the help he needs. This process should always involve a lot of prayer.

4. *Feed Trust*—Start feeding trust by rejecting gossip. But don't stop there; continue growing an environment of trust. When someone shares something in confidence, pray for the situation and then follow up with that person. A simple phone call or pulling that person aside when you see him goes a long way. In an overly macho culture, simple acts of caring are often lost. Don't mistake caring for weakness; it is actually quite the opposite.

DAY .4

Dear children, keep yourselves from idols.

1 JOHN 5:21

HAZARD:
ONLINE ABUSE

The past several years have seen a surge of online activity, especially in the world of social media like Facebook and Twitter. The positive effects associated with the rise of online social networking are vast, spanning from cultural and political revolutions to the fact that we can now easily keep up with friends. The Internet provides various platforms that are extremely advantageous to global outreach and have the potential for great good; however, as with any capacity for good, there is also the capacity for evil when abused. We must stress here that today's hazard is not the technology itself but the abuse of it and the by-products that result.

There is generally nothing wrong with participating in the social media world, but we must be aware of and avoid the hazards that come along with it. No doubt, the online social network is a community in itself, but what type of community is it? Facebook and Twitter allow us to shape and mold an image we want to show to the online community, obviously omitting the parts of our lives we believe to be undesirable. They also allow us to communicate with people without actually physically interacting with them. In some instances, people actually become bolder than they should, knowing there are little to no consequences for their online behavior. But the primary hazard here isn't cyberbullying, which is easy to spot and clearly wrong. The hazard of virtual communities is that, by definition, they are not real. There is a false sense of community.

Another hazard associated with online abuse is gaming. An inordinate amount of time can be spent on video games played online in a social context. Playing these games retains some elements of community in that it is a shared experience, one that simulates a safe environment by allowing people to interact without truly knowing one another. In these worlds, the gamer maintains a high level of control over his world and the people he interacts with. The games are designed to elevate the player to godlike status, no doubt the primary appeal and main reason for their wide popularity. There is nothing wrong with video games in general, depending on their content, but when the false sense of community begins to replace living in true Christian community, we have gone wrong. When other fundamental aspects of life (relationships and responsibilities) suffer because we spend obsessive amounts of time online, we must stop and regroup. After all, what do we gain from sacrificing true community for a video game? A beefed-up avatar? Think about it. The reality is that we will never be the men God has called us to be in the real world as long as we are wasting time in simulated realities. As J. Oswald Sanders said in his great book on leadership, "The young man of leadership caliber will work while others waste time."[2]

With the advent of the smartphone, a whole new means of taking in media was introduced. Now instead of leaving social media and gaming at home with a computer, we can carry it around in our pockets. One of the hazards to community the smartphone has exacerbated is texting. The danger lies not in the medium but in the abuse of it. Texting has become so commonplace that sometimes it interrupts, if not entirely replaces, face-to-face conversation. Doing the little things right is what matters in community. Ignoring an e-mail or message alert when involved in a face-to-face conversation goes a long way to show people you value them and their time. Pay attention to your phone habits; if you feel the need to check your phone, regardless of who you neglect in the process, some habit adjusting is probably in order. You're abusing your connectivity (or it is abusing you).

These online abuses cultivate a false sense of community, one that stands opposed to God's design for your life and the lives of those around you. Probably one or more of the abuses discussed has struck a chord in many of us. Here are some practical steps to take for regaining control.

FORCE MULTIPLIERS

1. *Scripture Memorization*—An idol is anything that we place more value on than God or what He intends for us. For some, the Internet is an idol that needs to be put down. Memorizing and meditating on verses such as today's Scripture will keep the truth in the forefront of our minds, bringing God's truth to bear when we're tempted to place more value on trivial things than we should.

2. *Accountability*—Online habits formed over a long period of time can be difficult to break. If you struggle to responsibly manage your time online, you might need to bring others in to help hold you accountable. Be honest about your online habits and discuss achievable goals with friends you trust; then decide on ways they can hold you accountable. If needed, most Internet filters have built-in timers that limit how long someone can spend online every day. This may be something to consider. We know this might seem extreme, but sometimes measures like this are necessary to kill old habits and cultivate the discipline needed to live in authentic Christian community.

3. *Fast*—The things you feed grow; the things you starve die. If you struggle with online abuse, it may be necessary to simply turn everything off for a period of time. Starving your habit will kill it. Not to say you should never be online again, but taking time off will allow you to clear your head and view your habits more objectively. Typically, when people return to normal following a fast, they are much more apt to put control measures in place to protect themselves from abuses. Even if you're not one to spend an exorbitant amount of time online, it is still a good idea to take a media fast

every once and a while for no reason other than simply to listen to the Lord.

4. *Practice Immediacy*—There is a term used in education called *immediacy*. It essentially means that people are actively involved in habits that bring them closer together. Some examples of immediacy are eye contact, disarming body posture or gestures (smiling or relaxed demeanor), focus on the other person's needs, and so on. We mention this because it is impossible to develop the type of closeness needed for the life change that occurs in authentic Christian community without immediacy. Immediacy is not possible online, and we devalue our time with others by paying more attention to a handheld device than to the people sitting across from us. Make time in your schedule to invest in the people around you. Practice immediacy. Let people know that you care by your availability—not just the quantity but also the *quality* of the time you spend with others. If you form habits that involve immediacy with others, you will find that the amount of time you spend online will naturally decrease.

DAY 5

A righteous man is cautious in friendship, but the way of the wicked leads them astray.

PROVERBS 12:26

HAZARD:
PEER PRESSURE

Over the last decade, our combined experience of mentoring and discipling young men has shown that the vast majority of people making destructive decisions do so based largely on their friends' influence. Insecure young men, those who have yet to establish a solid identity, are more likely to engage in harmful or illegal behavior so they will fit in and be accepted by a group of "friends." These so-called friends lack the maturity that comes from a grounded identity to begin with, so the blind end up leading the blind right into all sorts of destruction. The old cliché is true: Lie down with dogs, get up with fleas.

One of the most important decisions we make is our choice of friends. The community you choose will build you up or break you down; it makes good men better and bad men worse.[3] There is no way to avoid peer pressure. If we live around people at all, we will feel pressured to conform. However, it is our responsibility to determine who or what we allow to influence us. Who we choose to spend time with will determine what type of peer pressure we allow in our lives. If our core group of friends is made up of self-centered people who abuse almost everything from women to words, we are essentially inviting the same abuse into our lives. While we may have good intentions, it is far easier to be pulled down than it is to lift up. We are more likely to compromise our integrity when the only message we hear comes from godless friends living in a godless culture. This is negative peer pressure, the pressure that lures us into situations we normally would not agree to be a part of, inevitably resulting in consequences we aren't prepared for. And for what? So confused and insecure people will think we're cool? I'll pass—it's not worth it.

But just as negative peer pressure can tempt us to head down a destructive road, positive peer pressure can push us to do great things we never thought possible. A lot of people I know have a fear of heights, even if they don't admit it. This was clearly seen during my college summers when I worked at Kanakuk Kamps. With every group, we took our teenagers through the high-ropes course, and every time, it was a stark reminder of the power of positive peer pressure. Some people zipped right through and had a blast; others were pretty sure they were going to die. The thing that pushed those teenagers to face their fear and overcome it was encouragement from their friends. You could literally see the battle raging in their minds as they cautiously moved through the course. Fear was telling them to stop and get down, while their friends pushed them to take that next step and trust the ropes. Almost every camper completed the course. It's funny, the ones who feared the course the most had the greatest sense of accomplishment when they finished.

You will face circumstances in life so overwhelming it will make the high-ropes course look easy, but the principle is the same: If you surround yourself with the right people, they will make you stronger. Or to put it in the words of King Solomon, arguably one of the wisest and most accomplished men in history, "Though one may be overpowered, two can defend themselves. A cord of three strands is not quickly broken" (Ecclesiastes 4:12).

No one is meant to walk through life alone, but only you control who you walk with. Will you surround yourself with people who push you to be better every day or with those who blindly lead you toward harm and regret? You must choose.

FORCE MULTIPLIERS

1. *Scripture Memorization* — Peer pressure can be a powerful thing. We will all be faced with it to varying degrees throughout life, and each time, we need to be as well equipped as possible to discern whether it is positive or negative. We are most discerning and able to effectively repel negative peer pressure when we are familiar with truth from God's Word. Consistently memorizing and applying Scripture is the best thing we can do to skillfully navigate our culture and its pressures. It gives us the ability to not only reject negative peer pressure but also counter it and be a positive influence on those around us (1 Corinthians 10:13; Colossians 3:1-4; 1 John 2:15-17).

2. *Evaluate Your Friends* — Most people reading this should seriously evaluate their core group of friends. Do they follow Jesus? Do your friends take their faith seriously and encourage you to do the same? Do they consistently make wise decisions and avoid compromising situations? Are your friends willing to listen to healthy criticism and learn from their mistakes? These are just a few of the questions you should be asking about the core group of people you associate with. If the answer to these questions is no, you need to find a new group of friends. We are talking about the people you would consider your best friends, not acquaintances. Acquaintances are people you know and might be friends with, but they are not your inner circle. These people should not be held up to the same scrutiny as your core group of friends. You should unconditionally reach out to godless people, or how else will they know the gospel? You should also help encourage friends who are less spiritually mature to grow in their faith, but just don't allow these people to be the ones who influence you the most. Reserve those spots for guys who pursue Christ in every aspect of life. If your core friends look more like the world than they do Christ, some personnel changes are in order. Leaving a

group of people to find friends who will strengthen you is not easy; in fact, it may be very difficult. But dropping negative peer pressure and establishing positive influence is one of the wisest things you will ever do.

3. *Rehearse the Consequences*—When faced with negative peer pressure or the temptation to compromise what you know to be right, one of the best things you can do is rehearse the consequences of your actions. Most people don't think through things before they act, so they are left paying a price they weren't willing to pay. Every action has an effect; sometimes those effects are far-reaching and extremely painful, not only to you but to those around you. Considering the consequences of your actions may protect you from situations you will regret for the rest of your life.

AFTER-ACTION REVIEW

We all live in community. It is your responsibility to determine what type of community you live in. You can choose to settle for surface friendships that never challenge you to be a godly man, or you can choose to surround yourself with young men who live authentic lives as they pursue discipleship. The decisions you make in this area are some of the most significant of your life; they will shape the type of person you become. Who you choose to associate with will either drag you down or make you stronger. No one can make these decisions for you. You must choose. Just know that your choice of community should not be taken lightly.

True Christian community is hard work, but it is the most fulfilling investment of time and energy you will ever make. If done correctly, you will cultivate deep friendships that will last the rest of your life. Christian community is the primary instrument God has chosen to shape you into the image of His Son. By its very nature, it protects you from isolation, as a friend's unconditional acceptance challenges you to live life out in the open. It is an environment promoting maturity; conflict is consistently addressed in a healthy way, where forgiveness is sought and freely given. Friendship diligently guards against bitterness and anger, tactics of the Enemy that seek to supplant unity. Christian community cultivates an environment of trust as each member openly shares every facet of his life with brothers who care, with not just their words but also their actions. Men who live in true Christian community make time for each other and hold each other accountable to living lives set apart from the world.

Community is both a hospital and a gym. If you are hurting, your brothers will come around you and hold you up when you do not have the strength to stand. If you are weak in certain areas, they are the men who help you exercise the spiritual disciplines needed to grow. If you choose to do it God's way and go all in with your brothers in Christ, you will discover a strength and sense of purpose not known anywhere else.

We have both been blessed by quality friendships in every phase of life, finding this proverb to be true: "As iron sharpens iron, so one man sharpens another" (27:17). This is not an accident. Just as we have worked hard to make Christian community happen, we challenge you to be intentional about your friendships. Work to be the type of person that God uses to make it happen. Your life and the lives of those around you will never be the same.

Here are some questions to help facilitate discussion in your small group. Choose the questions from each day that stick out the most and discuss them as a group. Remember to be open and honest when answering and to give grace and mercy to those around you, as you will need the same from them.

Day 1: Isolation

1. Have you ever been in a crowd and felt alone? How did it make you feel not knowing anyone?
2. "True community occurs when we step out of our comfort zones and get serious about living life out in the open." How hard is it to be completely open with others? Do you have anyone you can be this open with?
3. What is your accountability partner's name? Do you consistently meet with this person and honestly share your life with him?

Day 2: Conflict

1. What is a conflict you have experienced? Tell the story. Do you believe you responded right or wrong in that situation?
2. What unresolved conflict is in your life? Do you need to ask anyone for forgiveness? How will you seek resolution based on what you've learned?

3. Do you think before you speak? Share a story about a time you put your foot in your mouth. How did that affect the people around you?

Day 3: Gossip

1. How do guys gossip? Give an example of how you gossiped about someone this week.
2. Has gossip ever hurt you? How does gossip break trust?
3. What should you do when you get in a situation where others are gossiping?

Day 4: Online Abuse

1. How many hours a day do you spend online or in some form of social media?
2. In what ways do you invest in other people? Does your activity online ever get in the way?
3. What benefit do you think there is to fasting from media? What difference do you think it would make in your walk with Christ?

Day 5: Peer Pressure

1. One popular statement says, "You become like the people you hang out with." In what ways is this true in your life? Is it true in your friends' lives? How?
2. When is the last time you gave in to peer pressure? What happened? What could have made a difference in that situation?
3. Do you think through the consequences of your actions before you act? Why is it wise to do so?

SELF-CONTROL

DAY 1

It is for freedom that Christ has set us free. Stand firm, then, and do not let yourselves be burdened again by a yoke of slavery.
GALATIANS 5:1

HAZARD:
ADDICTIONS

When most people think of the word addict, or addiction, certain things come to mind: drugs, alcohol, sex, adrenaline. Many people are locked in the grips of an addiction to substance abuse, most often in their own private world. When we hear stories of addiction, most of us think it is sad, some of us even feel pity for an addict's troubles, but very few of us realize the same condition that drove the person to the depths of addiction also exists in us. Although many people might never participate in the more socially taboo compulsions, the truth is that we are all susceptible to addictions, whatever form they take.

Our mistake is in thinking that the danger of addiction is the behavior itself, when the behavior is merely symptomatic of the deeper, real issue. These unhealthy behaviors are a perversion of something good. Most often, people start down the road to addiction because they want to be accepted or they want some relief from the pressures of life. Neither of these things is bad. There is nothing wrong with the desire for acceptance or the need for a break; often how we attempt to reach these things is where we go wrong.

Instead of finding his identity in his relationship with Christ, a teenager begins to abuse alcohol to be accepted by his friends. A person begins using drugs as a quick escape from a hard life instead of finding true rest in the sovereignty of God. The danger here is that our allegiance to the Lord is threatened and ultimately replaced by misguided attempts to fulfill desires only God can satisfy. In his book on love, C. S. Lewis describes the effect of replacing God as our greatest love: "We may give our human loves the unconditional allegiance which we owe only to God. Then they become gods: then they become demons. Then they will destroy us, and also destroy themselves."[1] The heart of addiction is loving anything more than we love God. The Lord is the only one qualified to be our master; He is the only one able to take our allegiance and give life.

Some might be tempted to not pay much attention to this hazard because they don't abuse drugs or alcohol. These same people might habitually view pornography or spend unhealthy amounts of time gaming online. Maybe they are consistently gluttonous, consumed with hobbies or so lazy they do nothing at all. The first step in finding victory over an addiction is to recognize you have one and then admit the need to change. Whatever addiction you struggle with, regardless of how it came about, it is time to change. It is time to give your ultimate allegiance back to the Giver of life.

Some may simply need to set boundaries to change a habit, while others have struggled with an addiction for so long that a dependency has formed and professional help is needed to overcome it. We must avoid the overspiritualized mistake common in religious circles that would have us simply "pray it away." Yes, of course prayer is always needed, especially in areas of intense struggle or hardship, but prayer is in addition to, not instead of, our own responsible action. Tough problems require tough solutions. Nowhere does it say that the Lord will give an easy road out. However, Scripture does tell us that we are not condemned (Romans 8:1) and that we are more than conquerors through Jesus Christ (Romans 8:37). Healing from addiction will take time, work, and maybe some professional help, but the Lord has promised to go with us and, as we keep our love where it belongs, see us to the end.

FORCE MULTIPLIERS

1. *Scripture Memorization*—The most crucial change that must take place in recovery is our thinking. We must replace the lies we believe with truth from God's Word. Memorizing Scripture on a consistent basis will strengthen you when faced with the temptation to give the love that rightfully belongs to God to someone or something else.

2. *Be Honest*—Some of you might have secret addictions and some have obvious addictions but are in denial about them. Either way, it is time to bring them into the light. There is no healing without confession (Psalm 32:5; James 5:16; 1 John 1:9), so step out of hiding or denial and find healing in the grace of God. It is a good idea to confess to a trusted friend or leader; as always, be wise about who you confide in. Telling the right people is crucial in getting the help you need.

3. *Community*—Getting involved in a community will provide accountability and the wisdom from others you need to set healthy boundaries. In some cases, a more focused and structured community for overcoming addictions through faith-based accountability (such as Celebrate Recovery or Life Hurts, God Heals) is appropriate. It is extremely rare to see someone recover from an addiction outside of community. This is a crucial step that may be intimidating at first but is worth taking!

4. *Keep a Biblical Perspective*—We must approach addictions holistically and address the situation from physical, emotional, and spiritual standpoints. Prayer must drive the recovery process but sometimes counseling and physical changes are needed depending on the addiction. If medication is needed, don't be afraid to comply with a doctor's orders; when used correctly, modern medicine can be an agent of God's grace.

DAY 2

Anyone who looks at a woman lustfully has already committed adultery with her in his heart.

MATTHEW 5:28

HAZARD:
PORNOGRAPHY

Sex sells, so it is literally everywhere, and it sells for a reason: Everyone wants it. Sexually charged images are all over the place: on billboards as you drive down the street, in advertisements when you watch TV, on the sideline when you go to the game, at restaurants where you eat, and above the urinal when you use the restroom. And that's before you even get to the Internet, where sexually charged content grows exponentially. Statistics show that 40 million people view pornographic websites every day, around 14 percent of the American population. Of those 40 million, 70 percent of men ages eighteen to twenty-four view pornographic websites in a typical month. Of all the days in a week, the most popular day to view porn is Sunday.[2]

Our culture has so engrossed itself in sex that the lines have blurred as to what is morally acceptable, something that has had a profound influence on the church. The Barna Research Group published a study on moral standards and found the following:

> Half of all adults stated that watching a movie with explicit sexual behavior is morally acceptable. That view was shared by three out of ten born again adults. In like fashion, more than four out of ten adults (43%) claimed that reading magazines with explicit sexual pictures and nudity is morally acceptable. Half as many of the born again adults embraced that perspective (21%).[3]

Sex is good. It was designed by God for our pleasure as an act of intimacy and is encouraged by God for those committed in a heterosexual marriage (Song of Songs 5:1). Scripture prohibits sexual promiscuity (1 Corinthians 6:18) not to be a killjoy but because the Lord knows the destructive power of sex when it is practiced outside of His intent. Sex is like a fire: When it stays in the confines of the fireplace, it gives comfort and warmth to the whole house. If it gets out of the fireplace, though, it burns the house down. Thus the need for self-control. God created us with a passion for women, something that serves us well in our pursuit of a wife and family; however, that desire can easily be directed toward all women and quickly move outside the confines designed for our safety.

When we give sexual desire godlike status, it becomes a demon and eats away at our soul. When this happens, we must take whatever measures necessary to kill it—not temper it or tone it down but kill it. The primary way to kill a sexual desire is to obey God. There is no other way around it. There is no shortcut or easier way; we must discipline ourselves for the purpose of godliness (1 Timothy 4:7b). The moment we bring our sexual desire under the lordship of Christ, it is placed where it belongs and becomes a great asset. True manhood is found not in our ability to embrace and exercise all our passions but in our tempering them and bringing them under the control of the Holy Spirit. The fact is that having many women doesn't reduce a man's sexual appetite; it excites it. It becomes an appetite that is impossible to quench; there is never enough. "The god dies or becomes a demon unless he obeys God. It would be well if, in such case, he always died."[4]

People delve into Internet porn on a computer at home, but the more subtle medium for viewing and transmitting pornography is the smartphone. People used to buy porn from a store, then it was accessible on a home computer, and now people carry it around in their pocket everywhere they go. Not only do people view pornography on smartphones, they also upload and send porn on them. "Sexting" is quickly becoming a popular way to send suggestive or pornographic pictures or videos through a text message.

Probably a vast majority of people reading this have at some point in their lives viewed pornography, whether they meant to or not. If you have elevated sexual desires to godlike status, now is the time to be honest: Do you allow lustful thoughts to linger in your mind? Do you view porn on the Internet? Do you use your phone to view or send porn? Do you watch pornographic movies or explicit content on TV? Have you been honest with a trusted friend or mentor about your sin? It is time to exercise self-control and build up the defenses needed to walk through life with purity. The following force multipliers and resources are great practical steps you can take to gain and maintain purity in a polluted world.

FORCE MULTIPLIERS

1. *Scripture Memorization*—There are some great passages in Scripture to commit to memory that will help in times of temptation (Job 31:1; Matthew 5:28; 1 Corinthians 10:12). If you continue to memorize Scripture, I guarantee that in vulnerable times, the right verses will come to mind.
2. *Accountability*—If you do not have an accountability partner, get one. The strongest ally you can have in the midst of this struggle is a brother in Christ. Make sure this person is mature enough to both show grace and speak truth that encourages you to get away from sin. This is a difficult balance to keep, but it is crucial. Make sure you cultivate this accountability relationship through consistent meetings and authentic conversations where both parties are completely honest.
3. *Filters*—Whether you view pornography online or not, we strongly recommend putting filters on every device able to transmit

pornography. This includes your personal computer, tablet, and phone. If we could make you do this, we would; it is that important. Neglecting to do so is evidence of bondage to sexual sin. Some good filters are X3 Watch, SafeEyes, Covenant Eyes, and BSafe Online.

4. *Guard Your Leisure*—In combat operations, it is important to identify and plan for the moments we are most vulnerable to attack. The same principle applies in our walk with God. Typically, during times alone or when we have very little to do, our minds tend to wander. It is in these moments that we are most vulnerable. There is nothing wrong with leisure, but if you struggle during these times, plan for a buddy to check up on you or plan an activity with friends. Don't let inactivity be a contributing factor to sexual sin.

Flee the evil desires of youth, and pursue righteousness, faith, love and peace, along with those who call on the Lord out of a pure heart.

2 TIMOTHY 2:22

HAZARD: MASTURBATION

Webster's dictionary defines lust as "unbridled sexual desire." Unbridled, unrestrained, out of control. There is a difference between a healthy sexual appetite and one that is unbridled. Unrestrained sexual desire quickly goes rogue and takes on a life of its own, wreaking havoc everywhere it goes. It doesn't help anything that our culture encourages everyone to break free from anything that might resemble sexual restraint. Ironic that the same culture that pushes sexual liberty is puzzled when the very thing it celebrates leaves a path of destruction in its wake. Young men of God must possess wisdom to navigate a sex-crazed culture unscathed.

Masturbation is a sensitive topic among Christians. For a long time, it was rarely talked about, and now that it is, there are a variety of stances across the spectrum, all held by people committed to the Lord. Some take a hard-line stance and teach that masturbation is always wrong, while others throw all caution to the wind and fail to recognize even the slightest danger associated with it. There is tension here because Scripture is silent on the matter, but there are principles from God's Word that can help us find a balance.

To help us tackle this subject, we will break it into two life stages: self-discovery and young adulthood. We'll take on the self-discovery stage first. Obvious changes occur to a boy's body when he goes through puberty, but there are psychological changes taking place as well.

Around the time they become teenagers, boys typically become sexually aware and are suddenly keenly interested in the young ladies around them. Unfortunately, at a time when a boy needs guidance for healthy sexual development, he most often finds himself trying to figure everything out alone. A boy's growing sex drive naturally leads him to explore his body and ultimately engage in masturbation. It has been joked that 98 percent of boys engage in masturbation and the other 2 percent lie about it. Masturbation in the self-discovery stage is typically separate from self-gratification as a result of lust and should not be condemned.

The young-adult stage is by far the more prevalent context for masturbation. When a young man develops into sexual maturity, his drive for sex will naturally push him to fulfill it. Not only does he notice a young woman's body but he becomes tempted to obsess about it. When he shifts from an appropriate appreciation for a woman's beauty to an unbridled desire for her body, he has moved into the realm of lust, and this is sin. When a young man begins undressing a woman in his mind and obsesses about what he would like to do with her, his sexual desire is rushing out of the confines God intended to protect it. To feed his desire, he will typically keep a mental picture of what he has seen and then masturbate for the sole purpose of gratifying his lust. He has objectified a young woman made in the image of God for his selfish desire. This is what happens most of the time, and it is always wrong.

The real struggle in keeping lust in check is what we do when the thought enters our minds. When we encounter a beautiful woman, our minds will naturally take notice. There is nothing wrong with this; it is evidence of our humanity and should be appreciated. However, the split second between appreciation and lust is the time we decide whether we will show self-control or not. The more we train ourselves to appreciate beauty and then move on, the stronger our resolve will be to keep lust at bay. The more we objectify women and allow our sexual desire to run wild, the more we will engage in self-gratification, something that can create a significant amount of heartache and dysfunction later in life when we enter a marriage relationship, not to mention the damage it causes to our fellowship with God.

Masturbation is about as universal a behavior among young men as there is.[5] We guarantee that a vast majority of the people reading this will struggle with masturbation to varying degrees. There is no quick cure, no fast fix, only the discipline of making wise decisions in the little things, those split-second decisions that determine the path we will take. Quite a few have consistently made poor decisions in this area, and some might even be addicted to masturbation. If this is you, don't despair. Through God's grace, pick yourself up and focus on making the next split-second decision for the glory of Christ. God calls us to purity — purity of intent, purity of mind, purity of heart. The journey is not a clean one, but through the power of the Holy Spirit, we can bring our behavior into conformity with who God made us in His Son.

FORCE MULTIPLIERS

1. *Scripture Memorization* — It is imperative that you spend time with the Lord daily and memorize His Word. You will have lustful thoughts; you will be tempted to objectify women and gratify your lust — these things are certain. The trick is to transform your thinking by renewing your mind with God's Word every day (Romans 12:2). The more Scripture you memorize, the better you'll get at this. The following verses address sexual purity: Job 31:1; Matthew 5:27-29; 1 Corinthians 6:18; 10:13; Ephesians 5:3; Colossians 3:5; 1 Thessalonians 4:3.

2. *Accountability* — You need a friend in your life who will ask you the tough questions. Set aside a time once a week in which you meet with that friend and the two of you ask each other some questions: "What did you look at this week on the Internet? If dating, were you and your girlfriend in any tempting situations this week? How is

your thought life? Have you masturbated this week?" The people
you surround yourself with will influence how far your lustful
thoughts go. Remember, lie down with dogs, get up with fleas.

3. *Bounce the Eyes*—Our culture feeds us a steady diet of sexual temptation and explicit images. Sex draws us in faster than anything. You
must develop a habit that when you see "that girl," you discipline
yourself to look away to something else, close the window, click off
the picture. Lingering draws you into lust, and it happens in a split
second.

4. *Build Fences*—Be sure every Internet device you use has a filter on it
to keep you from sexually explicit websites. Avoid environments that
stimulate lust. It is hard enough to fight this battle without putting
yourself in a situation where lust is all around. Get rid of anything
that might harbor lust. This might mean you have to hide or delete
a friend online simply because of the suggestive comments or
pictures shared.

Do not arouse or awaken love until it so desires.
SONG OF SOLOMON 2:7B

HAZARD: PREMARITAL SEX

Sex is awesome. God designed it that way. As its Creator, God gave us sex to be a sacred union between husband and wife. He commands in His word to take pleasure in your wife, to find satisfaction in her body and get drunk on her love (Proverbs 5:18-19). He is the one who gave us the Song of Solomon, a book so sexual that tradition holds that some rabbis prohibited its reading until a man reached a mature age. In seminary, one of the assignments in my Hebrew class was to translate the Song of Solomon. After a discussion on the sexual nature of the book, my professor joked that he knew where all the married students were going and encouraged all the single students to take a cold shower. Sex is good. God says it's good; the Bible says it's good. There is no doubt it's good.

Sex is only good, though, if left in the context God created it for, namely, heterosexual marriage. As we've discussed this week, when sexual desire is placed above obedience to God, it causes all sorts of dysfunction, from pornography and sexting to habitual masturbation and sex outside of marriage. Sadly, in our sex-crazed culture, we have disciplined ourselves to indulge our flesh, not control it, resulting in all sorts of social problems, such as teenage pregnancy, abortion, and sexually transmitted diseases. The fact is that seven out of ten have had sexual intercourse before age nineteen.[6]

Most young people believe that the traditional Christian view of sex is repressive and keeps them from having fun. I wonder if these people have really thought things through? Have they dealt with the drama and emotional turmoil? Have they counseled a pregnant teenage girl scared out of her mind? Have they been there when a young woman chooses to take the life of her child and walked with her through the guilt and shame that inevitably follows? Did they hear the pained regret in the voice that told his fiancée she won't be the only one? Have they tried to provide encouragement to the life that will never be the same because of a sexually transmitted disease? Have they heard the cry of the young woman used for sex and then abandoned? I doubt it. You slap a child's hand away from the stove because you know the stove will burn it. While the child might think you are repressive and ruining his fun, things look different from the adult's perspective. Maybe God built the fence up around sex for our own protection; have you ever thought of that?

The advice given in the Song of Solomon is profound: Do not wake up love until it is time. There is a time and a place for sex, and that is marriage. If you are single, abstain from sex, and do so with the knowledge and faith that God has your best interests at heart and that He will send the right person your way, someone who will awaken love as it is intended.

According to statistics, around 70 percent of guys reading this have engaged in premarital sex. Maybe you slept with your girlfriend before you became a Christian, or maybe you are a Christian and rebelled against God in this area of your life. Maybe you are not yet a Christian. It is possible that some of you have seen firsthand the negative effects of premarital sex we've mentioned. Wherever or whoever you are, lay your burden down. Jesus said, "Come to me, all you who are weary and burdened, and I will give you rest" (Matthew 11:28). The only place you are able to find the grace to move beyond your failure is at the foot of the cross. Jesus makes all things new.

FORCE MULTIPLIERS

1. *Scripture Memorization*—The Scripture you commit to memory is tucked away, ready for recall at a moment's notice when you're faced with the temptation to reach for the stove. Some great passages besides today's verse are: 1 Corinthians 6:18-20; 10:12; 2 Timothy 2:22.

2. *Establish Standards*—Think through what you will and will not do with a girl before you go on a date. If you are trying to make a decision while making out with her, it's too late. Some guidelines to cultivate sexual purity in your life are:

   ▶ Never get horizontal.
   ▶ Always set a time for the date to end, and have a buddy call to check that the date is over.
   ▶ Never go into each other's bedroom. Beds typically do not encourage purity.
   ▶ Never send text messages you wouldn't want her dad to see or read.
   ▶ Never video chat at night. Clothes have a tendency to come off at night.

   As the man of the relationship, it is your responsibility to sit down with the girl you are dating and communicate to her that you want to treat her with the respect and honor she deserves. If she does not respond well to the standards, she is probably not worth your time.

3. *Have a Plan*—In the Old Testament, a man named Joseph was faced with the temptation to have sex with his master's wife. He didn't think about it or consider whether it was a good idea; he simply ran away. Think through your plan for avoiding the temptation to have sex outside of marriage. Your plan should involve getting completely away from temptation.

4. *Rehearse the Consequences*—Start by asking whether or not the decision to engage in premarital sex is the best for your future. The choices we make today have consequences tomorrow.

5. *Accountability*—There is strength in numbers; two is better than one. Have a faithful friend call you on or after a date and ask direct questions: "Are you in a compromising situation? Have you remained pure?" It's funny how effective these tough questions can be to keep you out of a tight spot.

DAY 5

*No man can tame the tongue. It is a restless evil, full of
deadly poison.*

JAMES 3:8

HAZARD:
DESTRUCTIVE WORDS

The next time you're around a strong-willed child, pay attention to what he says. Often children are the most accurate picture of unrestraint available to us. They say some of the most hateful things to others. Anyone who said that children are innocent never met a child. With time, and hopefully some good parenting, some of the hateful speech is tempered, but it never fully goes away. As adults, we still wreak havoc with our words; they just might be more mature and creative.

Hurtful words said out of anger or careless words spoken without thinking will literally suck the life out of someone. This is so common that all of us have experienced the pain of a sharp tongue in some way. In defense, some people isolate themselves to avoid being hurt again, and in extreme cases, they suffer such intense pain and rejection from others that they take their own lives to escape. But just as words have the power to take life, they also have the power to give it. You may notice that some people are energized and light up from hearing just one encouraging word. Some become emotional and break down to tears because they rarely, if ever, receive an encouraging word or have someone actually believe in them.

Most of the time, people who use destructive words do so out of insecurity developed over time because parents, siblings, or authority figures consistently put them down. In turn, these people spread destructive talk to others like a disease, primarily because it is all they know; no one has ever come alongside them to teach encouragement. You may be one of these people. Encouraging others may be difficult or feel unnatural, but we must choose: Either tear down people with our words or build them up. One is easy to do; the other takes intentionality and skill. An encourager is someone whose identity is firmly rooted in Christ. He is confident in who he is and, therefore, does not feel the need to tear others down to feel better about himself. He is either naturally sensitive to those around him or has disciplined himself over time to be so. He pays attention to the needs of others and gives the right encouragement at the appropriate time. Because he is secure in Christ, he celebrates the accomplishments of others and is a steady encouragement for those in difficulty. He rejoices with those who rejoice and weeps with those who weep (Romans 12:15).

God, who encourages the downhearted, has called us to harness the power of the tongue and use it for His glory and the encouragement of others (2 Corinthians 7:6; 1 Thessalonians 5:11; 2 Thessalonians 2:16-17; Hebrews 3:13). We must evaluate ourselves and determine whether we use our words to build up or destroy. If we are encouragers, we must help others become so; if we consistently use words to destroy, we must change. God has given us the opportunity to affect the people around us and in some cases to completely turn a life around not only because we show we care but because we say it.

FORCE MULTIPLIERS

1. *Scripture Memorization*—Memorizing God's Word will give you the tools you need to catch yourself if you are discouraging or are blatantly mean. In moments of weakness, the Holy Spirit will bring to mind the truths you hide away in your heart. Don't slack in your discipline to commiting the daily verses to memory.

2. *Encourage*—No matter your experience with others, whether you've been around people who encourage or discourage, you can make a

conscious decision to be an encourager. Some might try to excuse themselves because people, maybe even people who were supposed to love them, have said extremely hurtful and hateful things to them their whole lives. It doesn't matter; we all are responsible for our actions, not the actions of others. Don't let someone else's failure cause you to fail. Break the cycle of discouragement. Embrace the fact that God believes in you and then believe in everyone else.

3. *Think Before You Speak*—Sometimes we intentionally set out to hurt people with our words; more often, though, we unintentionally wound others with our words simply because we fail to think before we mouth off. Discipline yourself to think of the effect your words will have on others around you before you speak. If you struggle with a loose tongue, it is a good idea to have a trusted friend hold you accountable for the words you say.

AFTER-ACTION REVIEW

Life often feels out of control. The overwhelming effort we exert to maintain a sense of control over the world—all the while ignoring the simple fact that no matter what, we are not God—can be exhausting. In coming to grips with this reality, there are only two appropriate responses. First, we must acknowledge that control belongs to God, and, second, we must submit to His will. After all, the only control we are instructed by Scripture to embrace is this second response of submission: self-control.

The discipline of self-control is absolutely essential to becoming a man of God. If we do not learn to control the self, we naturally drift toward "sexual immorality, impurity and debauchery; idolatry and witchcraft; hatred, discord, jealousy, fits of rage, selfish ambition, dissensions, factions and envy; drunkenness, orgies" and stuff like that (Galatians 5:19-21).

This week we put a strong emphasis on showing self-control in the area of sexual purity because of the onslaught of sexual temptation faced today. Dietrich Bonhoeffer describes this in his book *Temptation*: "In our members there is a slumbering inclination toward desire, which is both sudden and fierce. With irresistible power desire seizes mastery of the flesh. All at once a secret, smoldering fire is kindled. The flesh burns, and is in flames."[7] Allowing the fire to escape the hearth in any area of life is damaging, but in the area of sexuality, the destruction can be total. We must get this right. If we do not subject our desires to the will of God, they cease to be desires; they become demands. If we do not control our flesh, it controls us. There is no middle ground: Either we master them or we are enslaved.

Today's young man of God exhibits self-control in the midst of an out-of-control culture. He is the one who disciplines himself to bring his desires under the leadership of Christ. Because he is grounded in truth, he is equipped to recognize the dangers of allowing any desire to master him. He consistently rejects the temptation to give in to his flesh, but he is not perfect. When he does stumble, he confesses his sin to trusted friends and lives his life in the light. He is aware of his strengths and weaknesses and is committed to putting appropriate boundaries in place for his own protection. This is the standard. In a world filled with selfish indulgence, we are in desperate need of young men to swim against the stream. We challenge you to step up and be one of those men.

I have found that the more I discipline myself to submit to the Lord, the more I realize I am not in control and the greater I rest in the fact that I am not. The test of our trust comes in the difficulty, in the heaviest days when temptation is the strongest. In those days, let us remember that our lives are held firmly in the strong hands of the Savior and that no one nor anything can take us out of His hands (John 10:29). Let us draw near to Him and find that He is entirely trustworthy. He has shown Himself faithful to generation after generation of those who call on His name (Psalm 145:3-7). May our lives be worthy to join the multitude who have gone before us and found life is secure only in Him.

Here are some questions to help facilitate discussion in your small group. Choose the questions from each day that stick out the most and discuss them as a group. We encourage you to be open and honest when answering and to give grace and mercy to those around you, as you will need the same from them.

Day 1: Addictions

1. What is the first thing you think of when you hear the word *addict*?
2. Have you noticed addiction tendencies in your life? What are you addicted to?
3. What are some practical steps you can take to heal from your addictions? Who can hold you accountable to take these steps?

Day 2: Pornography

1. When do you find yourself most vulnerable to lustful thoughts?
2. When is the last time you viewed pornography? We said in the lesson to be honest with a trusted friend or mentor. Now is the time. Be honest!
3. What steps are you taking to protect yourself from the temptation to view pornography?

Day 3: Masturbation

1. What needs to change in your life in order to set healthy boundaries, preventing the split-second transition from recognizing beauty to objectifying young women?
2. "The journey is not a clean one, but through the power of the Holy Spirit, we can bring our behavior into conformity with who God made us in His Son." What does this mean?
3. Is masturbation right or wrong? What makes it right or wrong?

Day 4: Premarital Sex

1. In what context is sex great? What dangers exist outside of that context?
2. What happens when the desire for sex is put above obedience to God? How do we keep obedience our number-one priority?
3. What are standards you believe you should have with a girl? How should you talk to her about those standards?
4. What are good ways to romance a girl without the goal of any sort of sexual relationship?

Day 5: Destructive Words

1. When is the last time you witnessed someone hurt with words? (This could be in person or online.) What was your response?
2. What are some examples of how we don't think before we speak? What can we do to change this?
3. What are practical ways you can encourage and build up the people around you?

COURAGE

DAY 1

Fear not, for I have redeemed you; I have summoned you by name;
you are mine.

ISAIAH 43:1B

HAZARD:
FEAR

Toward the end of my time in Afghanistan, one of my sergeants informed me that an Afghan man wanted to talk to me at one of the entrances to our combat outpost. Wanting to get our Afghan counterparts more involved in their own country's conflict, I told the Afghan Army commander to go resolve the local's issue. He came back and told me that the local insisted on speaking with the American commander. Thinking there was something that needed immediate attention, I strapped on my sidearm and went to meet the man. When the local national approached me, I was partially exposed in the entry control point. When he reached me, I didn't get two words out before a rocket-propelled grenade flew directly over my head, missing our sentry truck by a few meters. When something that loud and sudden occurs, the first natural physical response is a heightened awareness of the danger around you—or fear.

There is nothing wrong with fear itself; in fact, many times it acts as a trigger that keeps us alive. As long as fear remains in its place, it proves to be a powerful ally. This can be a difficult thing to do, though, because most of us don't really trust the Lord. When our false sense of security gets threatened and we realize we are not in control, fear can paralyze us. This may result from a decision or desire to step out of a comfort zone into a new stage of life. It could involve losing a relationship you value or the possibility that you may never have the relationship you really want. Maybe it is simply the unknown, whatever the circumstance. When we choose to cling to self-dependence and our attempts to manipulate or control a situation instead of trusting God and releasing our fears to Him, we are giving fear more power than it deserves. The result is consistent worry about things we have no control over.

When we choose to take our focus off the Lord and put it on the shaky circumstances around us, fear begins to work against us (Matthew 14:30). We all experience times when we take our eyes off Jesus, leaving us a decision to either give in to our fear or release it to the Lord. It is what we do in these times that matters most. In traumatic situations, most people who give in to fear simply stop, or freeze up. This is the absolute worst thing we can do. By not taking action, we can become a liability to someone else—someone who may need us to take action. In everyday life, giving in to fear will tempt us to freeze up and stop moving forward. This may look like someone withdrawing from community or cutting off friends. It may be that a person lets an opportunity pass because there is risk involved, or a young man fails to pursue a young lady because he's been burned in the past. People who consistently give in to fear and never learn to step out in faith, despite the risks, end up living a life marked by indecision and regret.

The other option for dealing with fear is to give it over to the Lord. Giving our fear over to the Lord is a conscious choice we must make to trust Him. This is where many of us give lip service to trust; we say we trust Him, but we remain paralyzed in fear, waiting for Him to make something happen on our behalf. This is not trust. Trusting the Lord always involves action. Trusting God means moving forward with what we know to be true through His Word. For example, at times fear can be so powerful that we will doubt the sovereignty and goodness of God. It is in exactly those moments that we must choose to believe His Word. If Scripture is true (and we believe it is), then it is true all the time, regardless of our circumstances or how we feel about it. If fear tempts us to believe something contrary to Scripture, we must change. Trusting God is intensely practical; it is believing what is true *and* moving forward.

Proverbs 28:1 says, "The wicked man flees though no one pursues, but the righteous are as bold as a lion." We can either allow fear to paralyze us or we can trust God and move out, bold as a lion. There is no easy way; we must choose. Just know that the choice will determine what type of men we are—either men so consumed with fear that we jump at our own shadow, or men so consumed by the Holy Spirit that we stand boldly in the face of fear as we actively trust Him, knowing that the Lord is working everything for our good and His glory (Romans 8:28).

There is a two-word saying I cannot repeat here that most infantrymen use to express the selfless resolve to move forward under fire and complete the mission. These men understand fear as most never will, yet they have conditioned themselves to face their fear and move out. While their trust is often misplaced, the principle is the same. We need men today with such deep trust in the Lord that they selflessly move forward in obedience—men who contain their fear and use it as an ally, embracing only the fear of the Lord.

FORCE MULTIPLIERS

1. *Scripture Memorization*—This is absolutely crucial in keeping fear contained. Fear is a natural human response the Enemy constantly tries to exploit. When fear hits us, we are susceptible to Satan's lies about God and about our circumstances. Memorizing God's Word is our first line of defense against these attacks. It keeps us grounded and gives us the ability to combat the Enemy's lies with the truth. Not committing Scripture to memory is like going on a mission without your weapon.

2. *Community*—Christian community is totally unique. Although it may look similar to those who rally around one in need, it is different in how it gives assistance. When we face fear, our friends support us, pray for us, and arm us with truth to keep the lies of the Enemy at bay. That is the Christian way. There have been times in my life when I was afraid and susceptible to believing lies. The Lord used

my community to support me, holding me up when I did not have the strength to stand. These are the people sent to be the hands and feet of Jesus. Find friends like this and cultivate those relationships.

3. *Keep a Biblical Perspective*—When faced with uncertainty or fear, most of us try to get to a safe place as soon as possible. Sometimes, though, the Lord brings these fears and uncertainties into our lives to train us to trust Him. If we have the right perspective, we are able to embrace these times as opportunities for growth instead of something to run from. The promise is not that we will experience a life without fear but that He will give us the strength to stand firm in the midst of it (Isaiah 43:1-2; John 17:15; James 1:2-4).

DAY 2

I will give her back her vineyards, and will make the Valley of Achor a door of hope.

HOSEA 2:15A

HAZARD: REJECTION

God created men with an innate desire to matter, to do something significant and contribute to the world around them. Little boys grow up wanting to be someone strong, willing and able to save the day if called upon. When Brian's daughter, McKenna, got picked on at Chick-fil-A, his five-year-old son immediately came to her rescue. Boys want to be the hero. As time passes, this desire is at least tamed in most of us, if not destroyed altogether, as we feel the sting of rejection.

Rejection can come in various forms, from being picked last in a school-yard game to verbal abuse by a parent or authority figure to a cold shoulder from a certain young lady. Life is hard. Dreams die. Relationships are lost. Hearts are broken. Rejection is real, and it happens to all of us to varying degrees. How we handle it will make or break us.

It should come as no surprise that research shows that the fear of rejection is one of the top fears people face.[1] This fear is particularly powerful for men because rejection strikes us at our core human desire to matter, to make a difference, to be wanted and needed. Nevertheless, it is our choice how to respond to rejection, whatever form it takes. The fact that the fear of rejection is so common suggests that most people do not handle rejection very well and probably view it as an assault on their self-esteem. Those of us who allow others to define our self-worth are devastated by rejection. Being cut from a team may keep a person from trying out for anything again to avoid even the possibility of being rejected. The pain of being broken up with by a girlfriend might cause hesitation in pursuing someone else in an attempt to protect ourselves from more heartache. Having friends shoot down or even ridicule an attempt to share the gospel with them could make a person want to quit trying. As you can see, people who choose to allow others to define them end up being sidelined in the game of life each time they are faced with rejection. Assurance is replaced with insecurity over time. Nothing earth-shattering will happen. In fact, nothing will happen, and the one who cowers to rejection will slowly fade into passivity and insignificance. This is the most dangerous thing of all. But it doesn't have to be like this; there is another way.

A freshman named Josh was challenged to make a difference in his sphere of influence at school. He decided to step up and invite a friend to church. His buddy initially rejected Josh's invite. Instead of getting discouraged and avoiding a potentially awkward situation, he persisted to care for his friend and tactfully continued to invite him to youth functions at church. His buddy finally accepted the invitation and came to a youth event, where he was convicted of his condition apart from God and placed his faith in Jesus to save him. Because of Josh's persistence, his friend's life will never be the same. I'm certain his buddy is thankful Josh did not quit just because of a little rejection.

This is a small example of someone secure in Christ handling rejection properly. The situations you face may not look the same as Josh's, but the principle is the same: Young men grounded in Christ view rejection as an opportunity for growth. This does not mean it won't sting; it certainly will. No one in his right mind *wants* to be rejected. It does mean that painful circumstances in life are unique occasions for training in godliness and should be taken advantage of. In fact, there are times the Lord brings rejection into our lives either to protect us from putting ourselves into compromising situations or to bring about perseverance for the purpose of equipping us with everything we need (James 1:2-4). Coming to grips with the fact that rejection is part of life, especially the Christian life, is an essential quality for a leader. We will never be the men God intends us to be until we are able to handle rejection with courage, trusting in the sovereignty of God.

As followers of Jesus, we are told that we will be rejected by the world. If they nailed Jesus to a tree, what makes us think we will be treated any better? My dad used to tell me that if I wasn't experiencing some form of rejection by people far from God, then I was going the wrong direction. Many of you have probably experienced ridicule because of your faith, and that's in addition to the other types of rejection that are part of every person's life. Maybe you've allowed the pain of rejection to define you recently. Take heart: The Lord gives strength to the weak. In Him you will find the courage to face rejection with confidence and skill. The following steps are a great place to start.

FORCE MULTIPLIERS

1. *Scripture Memorization*—As with most hazards, the thing that makes them dangerous is not merely their existence but the opportunities they present the Enemy. Most often, the sting of rejection opens the door for the Enemy to come and do what he does best: lie. If we are not well equipped to counter his lies with the truth, his lies will run rampant and cause all kinds of insecurity and destruction. To discern the truth, we must commit Scripture to memory on a consistent basis. Keep at it.

2. *Evaluate*—When you experience rejection, take the time to do an honest evaluation of how you are handling it. Keep a consistent journal of your thoughts that you can go back to and reference. If the pain of rejection lingers and becomes overwhelming or debilitating, those are clear signs that you have allowed someone other than Christ to define your worth. Ask the Lord for the courage to face the pain and move on, and then pull trusted friends in close and allow your community to strengthen you.

3. *Take Risks*—Taking casualties is an interesting psychological process for combat units. Typically courageous men begin to hesitate and in some cases are incapacitated by the trauma of watching their friends get wounded or even die. Allowing men to linger feeds the fear and uncertainty, making it much worse. It is imperative for a leader to get his men back into the fight as soon as possible. It is the same with us. If you have been burned by rejection, don't linger. Get back out there and take a risk. Ask out that girl you've had your eye on, try out again, get up and move on. You'll find the situation you thought was an impossible Valley of Trouble (*achor* means "trouble" in Hebrew) is actually a Door of Hope.

4. *Learn to Laugh*—Captain Gerald Coffee, a man who spent seven years of his life as a prisoner of war in Vietnam, once said, "Laughter sets the spirit free to move through even the most tragic of circumstances. It helps us shake our heads clear, get our feet back under us, restoring our sense of balance and purpose. Humor is integral to our peace of mind and to our ability to go beyond the trivial." When used properly, humor is a healthy release. Learning to laugh at your circumstances and yourself lightens your load. It is evidence of an eternal perspective. In the grand scheme of things, the rejection you are facing is not as terrible as you might think. God can handle it—I promise.

DAY 3

Bless those who curse you, pray for those who mistreat you.
LUKE 6:28

HAZARD: GRUDGES

Have you ever had trouble forgiving someone? Maybe a friend talked behind your back or betrayed you, a girlfriend cheated on you, a coach or teacher was unfair, someone disrespected you—you were wronged. When this happens, especially if we did nothing to merit it, our natural inclination is to fight back. We may restrain ourselves from physically retaliating, but most of us have difficulty dealing with our anger and end up harboring resentment. Our bitterness inevitably turns into grudges against the offenders, grudges that can sometimes last for years.

There are two actions that damage: the actual offense and the grudge we choose to hold after the fact. The first is out of our control and only temporary. The second is self-imposed and brings the most harm, inflicting its damage as long as we allow it to. The only way to lessen the damage of the initial wound and avoid the destruction of grudges is to have the courage to forgive.

We don't pretend that the wounds don't go deep. Some people reading this have been on the receiving end of the worst kinds of abuse. Letting go of grudges and forgiving someone who has wounded you deeply is not easy; in fact, some of you are probably thinking it is impossible. Before we call it impossible, let's look at an example of forgiveness in the midst of injustice and injury. After being falsely accused of a capital crime and subjected to an unjust trial, a man was sentenced to death. Though his friends abandoned him and he was grossly mistreated, he had the vision to rise above the abuse and see the better way. Jesus forgave his executioners *while* they killed him (Luke 23:34). I sometimes wonder what amount of restraint it took to allow them to nail Him to that tree. Not only did He restrain Himself but He actually prayed for the man swinging the hammer. It is easy to feel anger and the desire to lash out, until I realize I *am* that man swinging the hammer. My sin put Him there. My filth made His sacrifice necessary. I am the one who betrayed Him: "While we were still sinners, Christ died for us" (Romans 5:8). When I am tempted to hold a grudge against someone, I remember that I have been forgiven much. It's funny how the people who grasp the depth of their own sinfulness tend to appreciate deeply the beauty of the gospel and are more willing to extend forgiveness to others. Grace has that effect.

No one said forgiveness would be easy, but it is not impossible (Matthew 19:26). There is really no other way. Either we release our grudge and forgive or we die inside. Holding on to grudges is like drinking poison and waiting for the offender to die. Grudges do nothing to the wrongdoer but are lethal to those who hold them. The initial wrong may have been someone else's fault, but allowing it to continue to affect you is on you. If you are holding a grudge against someone or grudges against multiple people, it is time to let them go, even if the person is unrepentant. Miroslav Volf sums this up well in his book *Free of Charge*:

> There's no question that it is more difficult to forgive when offenders refuse to repent. Their lack of repentance is, in a sense, a continuation of their offense in a different form. But the forgiveness is unconditional. . . . It is predicated on nothing perpetrators do or fail to do. Forgiveness is not a reaction to something else. It is the beginning of something new.[2]

Our world is in need of men who have the courage to walk down the road of forgiveness. Too many people are afraid to let go of their false sense of control and end up clinging to a grudge that drags them down into the depths of bitterness. What grudge are you holding on to? It could be directed at a friend, sibling, coach, or parent—maybe you refuse to forgive yourself. Whatever the case, it is time to grow up and show the maturity to embrace the forgiveness of God and extend that forgiveness to others.

FORCE MULTIPLIERS

1. *Scripture Memorization*—The hurt and pain that accompanies being wronged, especially by someone you trust, puts us in a dangerous spot. Our emotions can run wild, opening the door for bitterness to creep in. Often we even feel justified in holding a grudge against someone who hurt us. This is where memorizing God's Word is so crucial. G. K. Chesterton said, "We do not really want a religion that is right where we are right. What we want is a religion that is right where we are wrong."[3] One of the primary functions of Scripture is to correct us when we are wrong (2 Timothy 3:16). We are most easily corrected when we immerse ourselves in truth. When we fail to do this, we are more susceptible to walking the wrong road.

2. *Keep Short Accounts*—One of the most practical things we can do to keep from holding grudges is to cut them off before they take hold. This can be a difficult discipline to form, one that requires deliberate action. When someone wrongs you, make it a habit to address the conflict in a timely manner. This does not mean you have to stop everything immediately; you may need some time to process what has happened. It does mean that you do not let so much time pass that grudges begin to form. Go to the person who offended you and clearly communicate how you were hurt. Make sure to own any responsibility you may have in the situation. If he asks for forgiveness, forgive him. If he does not ask for forgiveness, forgive him anyway.

3. *Ask for Forgiveness*—Every time we feed our anger and hold grudges against people, we become just as guilty as the offenders. When we are hurt, it is difficult to take inventory and see that we are wrong; it

is much easier to play the victim. When there is conflict that leads to bitterness, we tend to demonize the offender and rationalize ourselves. Odds are that some of you have held grudges against people for a long time. Relationships have been broken and division exists where unity should, all because of the unwillingness to forgive. If this is you, take responsibility for your actions and own your grudge. Go to that person and ask for forgiveness, whether it is given or not. Don't give some general, halfhearted "I'm sorry." Make sure you name your sin and ask forgiveness for it; this is what shows genuine repentance and bridges the gap. It is extremely important that we stop playing the victim and own the fact that our grudge has dragged out an issue that should have been resolved a long time ago.

4. *Seek Counsel*—As mentioned previously, some of us have experienced deep wounds from unspeakable abuse. To move beyond this pain, we may need to seek counsel from a pastor or trusted friend. We may need professional help from a Christian counselor. There is nothing wrong with getting help when we need it. In fact, the only thing to fear is hanging on to the hurt. If you are having difficulty forgiving someone, get help so you aren't stuck in the prison of bitterness and resentment. Start with someone you trust and go from there.

DAY 4

Be on your guard; stand firm in the faith; be men of courage;
be strong.

1 CORINTHIANS 16:13

HAZARD:
SECULARISM

One of the consequences of being deployed in a combat zone is the heightened awareness that, for the most part, the world around you wants you dead. Living in this dangerous environment has a way of keeping you sharp. Because we live in a free society, I doubt many of us have had our lives threatened lately; however, each one of us is threatened every day by a society that is not simply indifferent to Christian belief and values but increasingly hostile to them. The strongest influence today is secular humanism, or the religion of self. The central theme of secular humanism's perspective is the absence of God: "We begin with humans not God, nature not deity. . . . No deity will save us; we must save ourselves."[4] Most people would not admit that they fit into this category, but our society promotes living life as if God were absent. They will tolerate those who live out their faith for a while, but ultimately they view us as harmful to human progress and will actively work to remove us from the public square. This is hostile territory for those of us following Christ.

The influence of secularism begins early and is seen in various mediums. For most of us, it starts with television or movies. In general, the media industry produces programs and films that encourage living a life opposed to what God intends. There is no way we can be daily exposed to a culture far from God and not be affected by it. The influence spreads as we enter the classroom and are consistently fed ideas that push for a life apart from God. Unproven theories are taught as fact and the Christian worldview is discounted to the point that Christians are presented as irrational and intellectually under-developed. This is the world we live in. As teenagers and young adults, you are in the process of shaping your belief system and are, therefore, the primary target in the war of ideas. Frankly, the evidence is showing that secularism is winning the fight, as more teenagers than ever are abandoning their faith at college.[5] You may have not yet realized that you are in a combat zone where two opposing ideas are competing for your life.

Far too many of us simply go with the flow of culture. We end up chasing what society says is important and live a life of self-indulgence, going to great lengths to be the best-looking or most athletic or most popular. For others, self-indulgence looks like the exact opposite, aban-doning these things altogether and taking pride in being lazy, not doing anything at all. Either way, we waste the God-given potential to make an eternal difference. We end up living lives that declare by our actions that God is dead.

It is time for us to stop approaching our culture like a wet paper sack and giving in at the slightest hint of pressure. We need young men will-ing to work hard to prepare themselves to defend their faith with skill in the public square. We need men willing and able to give strong, educated answers to difficult questions. Most of all, we need young men who are humble, patient, loving, kind, and wise. We need men whose lives reflect what they claim to believe. There is no promise of popularity or political correctness here. If you choose to step up, you will certainly face scrutiny and hostility, but at least you will be in the fight and not a victim of it. Train yourself to stand up for truth. Act like a man. Be courageous. There is so much "God is not" going on in our culture that someone needs to stand up and say, "God is."

FORCE MULTIPLIERS

1. *Scripture Memorization* — If our secular culture were a plane, it would fly upside down. The problem is that it thinks it is right side up. The heart of what you will be taught in our society is a direct inversion of Christian values. Of course, the only way to know this is to know what Christianity actually teaches, and to know that, you must know the Bible. There's no way around it. Memorize the Word.

2. *Evaluate Yourself* — Take a regular inventory of your life. Are you allowing yourself to be directly influenced by ideas contrary to Scripture? Are you someone who tends to go with the flow of culture, or do you realize that you are in a war of ideas? Do you consistently take a stand for truth, or do you cower down to avoid conflict? Do you feel equipped to answer challenges to your faith? How are you leveraging your influence with the people around you to teach the truth and glorify Christ? These are the types of questions we should ask ourselves on a consistent basis. Share your evaluation with a trusted friend or small group and have them hold you accountable to improving.

3. *Study* — Put down the gaming controller, turn off your phone and computer, and pick up a book. The best leaders are well read. The great thing about reading is that it allows us to engage with the greatest minds the world has ever seen. If you read a wide variety of works, you will get to know the author and the way he thinks, even if he is dead. Don't be afraid to read the classics, the books that have stood the test of time. This is crucial for our maturity. As Isaac Newton once said, "If I have seen further, it is by standing on the shoulders of giants." We have spiritual giants who have gone before us, willing to teach us if only we pick up their book and read. Why would you not do this?

4. *Have a Plan*—Most of us do not live intentional lives. We react to events that occur around us. There are three types of people: ones who make things happen, ones who watch things happen, and those who ask, "What just happened?" The ones who make things happen have a plan. All of us should look at the sphere of influence God has placed us in and ask, *How can I best utilize what God has given me to maximize my influence among my friends?* Once we have evaluated the situation, we should formulate a plan that is simple and measurable. It may be as easy as planning to share the gospel with a friend at lunch or as complex as organizing an ongoing Bible study or discipleship group. Maybe it is planning a prayer group. Making an eternal difference does not just happen; if you don't have a plan, get one.

DAY 5

God did not give us a spirit of timidity, but a spirit of power, of love and of self-discipline.

2 TIMOTHY 1:7

HAZARD:
TIMIDITY

A majority of popular shows on television today do not paint a flattering picture of manhood: emotionally compromised, effeminate males prancing around their high school; office bosses who are bumbling idiots and overly insecure; relationally distant dads who only care about beer, women, and football; and reality stars who literally cannot think of anyone other than themselves. Unless a young man has a strong, relationally connected father or mentor in his life (which is rare), the portrayal of masculinity in the media becomes his standard. The result is that many men are insecure, passive, and timid. The media's picture of masculinity falls tragically short, and many young men never have a healthy model of true manhood.

The biblical standard for manhood stands in direct contrast to the watered-down masculinity portrayed by the world. We need secure men of integrity who are self-controlled and accountable, men of knowledge and principle who courageously stand for the truth. We need men who are protectors and liberators. The Lord is consistently portrayed as one who actively promotes justice and takes a stand against evil. He encourages the afflicted and defends the oppressed (Psalm 10:17-18; 72:4). He is the ultimate Warrior Protector, and we are called to be like Him: "A warrior is one who possesses high moral standards and holds to high principles. He is willing to live by them, stand for them, spend himself in them, and if necessary die for them."[6] When was the last time you defended someone who could not defend himself? Have you ever stood your ground against those who assault your principles? When was the last time a righteous anger welled up inside of you because of injustice or abuse around you? Have you ever boldly taken a stand for the marginalized? This is what we are supposed to do; this is who we are.

It is time for us to reject the timidity that accompanies the world's view of manhood and embrace God's call for us as men. Instead of backing down, step up. When you see oppression or injustice around you, quit being a spectator and do something. If people around you are mocking your faith, stop pretending you aren't a Christian and take a stand. Don't be timid about who you are. Stop caring about being acceptable to a godless world and start caring about the expansion of God's kingdom. I wonder how many of us will look back at our lives and wish we had done less, not taken as many risks, or spent more time chasing trivial things. Probably not many. Timidity produces regret; don't settle for the meaningless life this world would have you lead: "You have one life. That's all. You were made for God. Don't waste it."[7]

The crest of the Green Berets reads *de oppresso liber*, Latin for "to liberate the oppressed." The last line of the Ranger creed describes how this occurs: "Readily will I display the intestinal fortitude required to fight on to the Ranger objective and complete the mission, though I be the lone survivor." Whether you are an actual military warrior or not, the principle is the same. Step up and liberate the oppressed, protect the vulnerable, stand for principle, defend your faith, show the guts to press on, be courageous, be a man—even if you stand alone.

FORCE MULTIPLIERS

1. *Scripture Memorization*—How are we supposed to know the attributes of biblical manhood if we don't know the Bible? Memorizing God's Word will give us the tools we need to discern between the world's standard for manhood and God's. It provides

recall for us in tough situations to draw strength from the truth and reject timidity, allowing us to take a strong stand for Christ.

2. *Do Guy Stuff*—Depending on our background, some guys struggle with a masculine identity. Instead of giving in to the effeminate portrayal of the modern man, try doing things associated with the traditional (but not secular) view of man. Go outside. Spend time in the wild. Go camping. Take a hunting trip with friends. Build, explore, climb, shoot—do whatever you need to do. Not everyone is the prototypical man, so don't try to be; however, each of us should proactively pursue activities associated with manhood. God didn't just make you a person; He made you a man. So man up.

3. *Challenge Yourself*—This is one of the most proactive things you can do to combat the world's emasculating view of manhood. Those who don't typically challenge themselves should start small and set achievable goals to avoid discouragement. Push yourself in every area of life. If you're afraid of heights, go cliff jumping. If you want to get crazy, go skydiving. If you need to lose weight, get to the gym or start running. If you feel unequipped to defend your faith, take a class on apologetics. If you are afraid to share your faith, formulate a plan to reach out to a friend who is far from God. Challenge yourself and finish what you start.

4. *Show Initiative*—"A man without initiative is not a man."[8] It is fairly accurate to say that if you don't do it, it won't get done. Stop waiting around for everyone else to do what you should be doing. When it is called for, be the first to act, the first to speak up, the first to defend, the first to protect. Step up and be the one to start a Bible study or accountability group.

AFTER-ACTION REVIEW

We live in Enemy territory. There are ideologies and influences all around us that are consistently assaulting the biblical standard for manhood. The Enemy has gone after the health of not only our society but also the church by projecting a standard that is passive, weak, and emasculated. More and more guys today have bought into the secular definition of manhood and are content to relinquish their responsibility to lead because they are too timid to assume the risk involved. The body of Christ is hurting for men of courage.

We need men unafraid of standing up to the powers that would tame us; men of courage who understand fear and who, instead of being controlled by it, use it to their advantage; men who move out in the face of uncertainty because they firmly believe that obedience to Christ is more important than personal safety. We need young men of God who implicitly trust the Lord and take advantage of difficult circumstances to learn from adversity.

The Lord is calling for men willing to forgive and overcome the bitterness. The body of Christ is in dire need of young men who don't settle for weak, cop-out answers to very real questions on Christianity but rather discipline themselves to put in the hard work needed to defend the gospel of Christ with skill in an arena that embraces foolishness. When will you decide to step up and join the ranks of those warriors who reflect the nature of God by defending the weak and liberating the oppressed? Now is the time. Give yourself fully to the call of the Holy Spirit and He will inject you with a courage you've never known.

Don't timidly become a male who merely takes up space. Be a man. Reject passivity. Embrace your role as a leader, regardless of the hazards.

The Lord is calling you to be a man who knows who he is and, in the power and strength of the Holy Spirit, courageously does what is right, even if it costs him his life. There are things worse than dying. We have our orders; let's move out.

Here are some questions to help facilitate discussion in your small group. Choose the questions from each day that stick out the most and discuss them as a group. As always, we encourage you to be open and honest when answering and to give grace and mercy to those around you, as you will need the same from them.

Day 1: Fear

1. What are you most afraid of?
2. How does fear slow you down?
3. What does fear do to your walk with Christ?

Day 2: Rejection

1. Have you ever been rejected? How did it make you feel?
2. How does it make you feel when you fail? Did failing at something make you timid the next time you were doing that same thing?
3. When you get knocked down, the challenge is to get back up. How do you get back up from your failures? When you are rejected, how do you recover?

Day 3: Grudges

1. What were some of your thoughts as you read about holding grudges?
2. Who do you need to forgive? Why do you need to forgive them?
3. Is it more difficult to ask for someone's forgiveness or receive someone's forgiveness? Why?
4. What does it mean to forgive yourself?
5. How does knowing that Christ has forgiven you change the way you see yourself and others?

Day 4: Secularism

1. What is the number one influence in your life? How does that influence shape you today?
2. Who is shaping your friends' views of the world?
3. What does it mean to have a "biblical worldview"?
4. List five attributes of a godly man. Why did you pick each one?

Day 5: Timidity

1. How does pop culture portray men today? How does that differ from biblical manhood?
2. What are the areas of life in which you are timid? How can you challenge yourself to overcome your timidity?
3. "A man without initiative is not a man." What does this mean?
4. What is some "guy stuff" you and some godly friends can do regularly? Other than being fun, what benefit might this have for you and your group of friends?

CHECKPOINT 6

PATIENCE

DAY 1

Man's anger does not bring about the righteous life that God desires.
JAMES 1:20

HAZARD: ANGER

We are created to be emotional people. Without going into formal psychological definitions, emotions are simply the things we feel, feelings that can (and usually do) produce some sort of response. Emotions can be unpredictable and come on in an instant. Probably the most common and potent emotion males experience is anger. Has anyone ever talked trash to you? Has someone ever lashed out at you or cussed you out? Have you ever found out people were talking behind your back? How do these situations make you feel? Angry? Me, too. What happened to your thought process when you experienced that emotion? It more than likely was blurred. Experiencing strong emotions tends to cloud our judgment, resulting in potentially hazardous reactions.

Just as with most hazards we have identified in this study, there is nothing inherently wrong with anger; in fact, there are times we are commanded to be angry. It only becomes a problem when it is out of control. Experiencing anger is not sin, but how we choose to react to it will make or break us. Whether or not we are naturally prone to anger, we all have a choice regarding what we do with it. Scripture is clear that anger resulting in bitterness, resentment, arguing, strife, jealousy, envy, or any sort of selfishness is sin (Galatians 5:20; Ephesians 4:31; Colossians 3:8). It warns against associating with a person who consistently gives in to the temptation to let his anger run wild and out of control, calling this person a fool (Proverbs 14:29b; 15:18a; Ecclesiastes 7:9). Like any sin, if we give anger an inch, it will run a mile. Uncontrolled anger will absolutely wreak havoc in our lives, leaving a wake of destruction in its path, from broken relationships to disqualification from leadership, even negatively affecting our mental health and sometimes our freedom. The key is to train ourselves to recognize anger and either release it to the Lord or turn it into fuel, mobilizing us for something good. After all, not all anger is bad.

First Corinthians 13 says that love is slow to anger; it does not say there is no anger at all. In His love, the Lord shows great patience, but His wrath does not allow injustice to go unpunished. Instead of selfish, reactionary, flash-in-the-pan anger, the Lord's anger always follows a prolonged period of patience, waiting for the rebellious to repent. Make no mistake: His patience does not last forever. His wrath will finally come as an act of righteous justice and will be total (Hebrews 10:31; Revelation 14:10). Although we will never be able to show the long-suffering that God demonstrates toward us, we are called to be slow to anger—as He is—and to bring our anger under the control of the Holy Spirit (James 1:19-20). This is a delicate balance we must master. We must respond with gentleness when we are the recipients of rage (Proverbs 15:1) and control our temper when provoked (16:32). We display wisdom when we overlook small offenses and are quick to forgive (19:11).

When encountering injustice, however, it is righteous anger that leads us to action. We are commanded to show anger when it is called for and intervene in unjust or abusive situations (Ephesians 4:26).[1] The anger you would feel from witnessing a criminal attack a helpless lady on the street *should* move you to act; it is a good thing. In such instances, we sin not if we are angry but if we are passive. Our sin would be our doing nothing. When Jesus saw the injustice of robbing worshippers in the temple courtyard, His anger led Him to drive out the embezzlers, cleansing the temple of impurity (John 2:15-17). Godly men exercise patience regarding human anger but act boldly against injustice when moved by righteous anger. Edmund Burke once said, "All that is necessary for the triumph of evil is that good men do nothing." The world needs good men, godly men, who know when and how to take action. We reflect the nature of God both in our patience and in the strength we show to confront evil.

FORCE MULTIPLIERS

1. *Scripture Memorization*—There are a handful of verses in today's lesson that directly address the issue of anger. Committing these to memory will allow us to call truth to mind when anger first hits and our judgment is clouded. Keep up this discipline; you are transforming your mind.

2. *Stop, Listen, Think*—Before you react to someone's fit of rage, stop. Take a step back and evaluate. Don't just hear what that person is saying; listen to him. Most of the time, anger is a veiled wound. If we discipline ourselves to discern the deeper issue, we will not only save ourselves a lot of heartache but also help a brother, or total stranger, in obvious need. Before you respond, think about the consequences of your actions, either bad or good, and move from there. "Be quick to listen, slow to speak and slow to become angry" (James 1:19).

3. *Actively Address It*—When you give in to the temptation to lash out in anger, make sure you actively address the sin as soon as possible. This means you must humbly go to the person or people you have wronged, confess your anger, and ask for forgiveness. Allowing your selfish anger to stick around is like feeding a cute lion cub: It's amusing and seemingly harmless at first, but then it grows up and devours you. Kill the anger before it ruins your life.

4. *Stay Away from Loose Cannons*—You guys know these types: people who snap and are furious at the drop of a hat. If you always feel like you're walking on eggshells around a person, he's probably a loose cannon. These are the people Scripture warns against: "Do not make friends with a hot-tempered man, do not associate with one easily

angered, or you may learn his ways and get yourself ensnared"
(Proverbs 22:24-25). Don't allow loose cannons into your closest
circle of friends; they will only cause problems.

5. *Get Angry*—If you experience personal injury, you are called to
turn the other cheek (Matthew 5:39). However, when it comes to
injustice or oppression occurring around you, righteous indignation
is called for. In our spectator culture, way too many of us stand by
and do nothing. This is unacceptable. If you are able to intervene to
stop injustice and oppression, your anger should drive you to action.
If it doesn't, something is wrong. Stand up for the marginalized,
helpless, and weak. It's what God does.

DAY 2

Why do you look at the speck of sawdust in your brother's eye and pay no attention to the plank in your own eye?
MATTHEW 7:3

 # HAZARD: FRUSTRATION WITH RELATIONSHIPS

When Brian was a kid, he got ticked off one day and told his parents, "I'm out of here. I don't need y'all." He proceeded to pack a garbage bag full of toys (no clothes, just toys) and walk out of the house. He only made it to the end of the street before he realized the absurdity of his little runaway. His frustration with his parents caused him to make a foolish decision. We laugh at stories like this, but we do the same thing; our frustrations and resulting foolish decisions are just a bit more mature. Our relationships bring us the most joy in life, but they also cause the most pain. We must learn to approach our relationships with a biblical perspective and be patient with others because we are all sinful.

Odds are you are experiencing frustration with a relationship right now, whether with a parent, sibling, coach, teacher, friend, or girlfriend. No doubt, the source of our frustration has to do with some sort of shortcoming on the other person's part. Someone has in some way not lived up to an expectation we had; maybe someone we'd hoped would change has not or someone we trusted and relied upon has disappointed us. Despite our best efforts, other people continue to frustrate our attempts to keep the world the way we think it should be. If only my friends could see it my way, if only my coach would realize my talent, if only my parents weren't so hardheaded . . . if only. The trouble with every problem or frustration we have with other people is that they are not the only actors in the drama. There is one common character in them all, the one we never see: me.

The key to handling our frustration toward others correctly is to do our best to gain and maintain the Lord's perspective. We tend to demonize others because their faults are glaringly obvious to us, but the Lord sees it all. He sees both their stubbornness *and* ours, their faults *and* ours. Just as others disappoint and frustrate, we also disappoint and frustrate, yet God forgives and loves us the same. The key to maturity in dealing with frustrating people is to "learn to see ourselves as a person of exactly the same kind."[2] That is what we are. We're no different, really. We all need God's grace and each other's. When we gain the Lord's perspective, we see that a vast majority of our frustration exists only because imperfect people are part of our imperfect expectations. The sooner we learn to hold things loosely and view frustrating situations as opportunities for growth, the easier it will be to see people as we want to be seen — accepted for who we are. When we realize this truth, we get closer to the heart behind Jesus' teaching to love our neighbors as ourselves (Matthew 22:39).

Nathan and his wife once had the opportunity to come alongside another couple with relationship problems. Neither person was perfect, but while the guy admitted his mistakes and was willing to change, the girl was convinced she was a victim who had little to no responsibility in their conflict. Despite multiple attempts by different people to address her unwillingness to take responsibility for her actions, she remained obstinate and simply quit the relationship, causing an enormous amount of pain. Until we are willing to take our eyes off everyone else's problems and focus on changing the one person we actually have control over, our lives will be marked by one frustrating relationship after another. It is time to stop waiting for everyone around us to change and to start becoming the change we seek. If you want to see everyone around you change, go to your room and start with the man in the mirror. Leave everybody else to the Holy Spirit. I think you'll find that your patience toward others will grow.

FORCE MULTIPLIERS

1. *Scripture Memorization*—Most of the time, frustration with relationships is a matter of perspective, and nothing changes perspective like Scripture. We are told that the Word of God "judges the thoughts and attitudes of the heart" (Hebrews 4:12). If our attitude needs to change, it is God's Word that will change it. Memorizing Scripture keeps us spiritually and mentally sharp, allowing us to move through hazards without becoming casualties.

2. *Take Responsibility*—If you find yourself always blaming things on other people or playing the victim, quit. Not every problem in our lives is somebody else's fault; in fact, very little is. Most of the time, we are the ones who did not work hard enough. We are the ones with the bad attitude. We are the ones who think everything should simply go our way. Stop feeding the growing sense of entitlement in our society and actually take responsibility for your actions. If a relationship has been injured because of an unrealistic or false expectation on your part, go to that person and own it. Make it right.

3. *Keep a Biblical Perspective*—I'm convinced that most frustration in relationships is the result of bad theology. We think we are much better than we actually are. A Christian who truly grasps sinfulness and grace, however, knows that the very things that drive us crazy about other people exist in us also. Every time we get frustrated at someone else, we are the pot calling the kettle black. If you find yourself consistently frustrated at others, take in a healthy dose of Romans 3:10-18. Be patient with others, as you'll need them to be patient with you, too.

4. *Low Expectations, High Flexibility*—When you understand human sinfulness, your expectations of other people will go way down. This is not a bad thing. I am rarely surprised when people around me make poor choices or things don't go my way. This is the way of

our fallen world. We're not suggesting you look down on others; just be realistic. Keeping low expectations allows us to be more flexible in an unpredictable world. We aren't crushed when other people disappoint us. Instead of getting angry or frustrated, this actually frees us to view others as hurting people in need of love and support, like us. Keep your expectations low and your quality of life will improve.

DAY 3

Consider it pure joy, my brothers, whenever you face trials of
many kinds, because you know that the testing of your faith
develops perseverance.
JAMES 1:2-3

HAZARD:
FRUSTRATION WITH GOD

Have you ever been frustrated with God? Maybe something you were
counting on didn't go your way or you lost something or someone of
great value to you. It could be that life has consistently thrown one hardship after another at you and naturally you wonder why. Christopher,
a junior in high school, shared with us a frustration most Christian
teenagers and young adults face on a daily basis:

> I have been frustrated with God before because I live for Him and try to be a
> light for Him, and I guess since I do that, I expect everything to go good, but
> that's not always the case. I get frustrated because people who go out on the
> weekends and party look like they are doing good, and life is great, and they
> don't have a care in the world. Everything is going right for them. The really
> good athletes just live life to the fullest, getting all the girls and letters from
> colleges, and at the same time, they are getting smashed on the weekends
> and doing drugs. I'm trying my best to live a life that glorifies God in every-
> thing, but on the outside, my life doesn't look as good or as fun as theirs.

Christopher's frustration finds itself in good company. Some 2,600
years ago, a prophet named Jeremiah expressed a similar but stronger
frustration: "O LORD, you deceived me, and I was deceived; you overpowered me and prevailed. I am ridiculed all day long; everyone mocks
me" (Jeremiah 20:7). Then there is Job, the one who had more reason to

be frustrated at God than any of us. He does away with the polite tone and cries out to God with brutal honesty:

> Now my life ebbs away;
>   days of suffering grip me.
> Night pierces my bones;
>   my gnawing pains never rest.
> In his great power God becomes like clothing to me;
>   he binds me like the neck of my garment.
> He throws me into the mud,
>   and I am reduced to dust and ashes.
> I cry out to you, O God, but you do not answer;
>   I stand up, but you merely look at me.
> You turn on me ruthlessly;
>   with the might of your hand you attack me.
> You snatch me up and drive me before the wind;
>   you toss me about in the storm.
> I know you will bring me down to death,
>   to the place appointed for all the living. (Job 30:16-23)

There is nothing wrong with being honest with God about how you feel. I promise, He can handle your questions and pain. The Bible is packed full of real people venting real feelings to a very real God. You just read where God let Job unload before putting him back in his place. The danger that accompanies our frustration with God is the temptation to abandon Him because of our pain. Two points here. First, we can learn from one of my favorite passages in the Bible. Jesus finishes teaching the crowd about the difficult realities of following Him. Many of the people leave when it isn't what they expected, but His disciples remain. He turns to them and asks, "You do not want to leave too, do you?" Peter answers him, "Lord, to whom shall we go? You have the words of eternal life" (John 6:67-68). That's right on. You may be tempted to leave, but where will you go? So we trust and endure.

Second, pain is not a bad thing. Think of all the great things that have happened in your life. I'd bet most, if not all of them, came through some sort of pain. Championships are not given; they are earned through a lot of hard work and physical pain. Academic success doesn't come through doing nothing; it is the culmination of a lot of long nights and focused effort. We don't learn to endure by feeling good all the time. We give pain a bad rap. It is the primary means for obtaining our most valuable traits: perseverance, empathy, forgiveness, even love. The human spirit is strongest when it has been tested in the fires of hardship and comes out unscathed. Do you really think the Lord doesn't know this? In our pain, He sees what we do not: the rough parts of us being transformed. Don't reject the pain.

There are no easy solutions to difficult, painful situations. One final lesson from Job: He was frustrated with God the entire time he was suffering, yet by the end of the book of Job, his complaints are gone and everything is restored. None of Job's questions was answered, nor did God give an account of why Job had to endure such pain. The Lord simply showed up and Job's frustration was put in perspective: "My ears had heard of you but now my eyes have seen you. Therefore I despise myself and repent in dust and ashes" (Job 42:5-6). I believe this is the key. When faced with difficult, sometimes overwhelming circumstances, our natural response is to try to make the pain go away. When it doesn't, we live in frustration. Perhaps the right thing to do is shift our focus off ourselves and onto the Lord. He has promised to walk through the hard times with us (Isaiah 43:1-2); we should trust that God is at work for our good and His glory—always.

FORCE MULTIPLIERS

1. *Scripture Memorization*—Knowing God's Word is crucial when encountering this hazard. We are never more vulnerable to the lies of

the Enemy than when we are in pain. The temptation for escape is already in place; one or two well-placed lies can convince us that a better life exists apart from God. The Enemy chose to tempt Jesus when He was physically weak, He will do the same with us. Just like Christ, though, our greatest defense against these lies are the words "It is written . . ." (Matthew 4:4).

2. *Be Honest*—There are people in some circles of Christianity who believe we should always come to God as though we have it all together. I have no idea why they believe this. God knows us better than we know ourselves. If we are ticked off at God, believe me, He already knows it. Drop the mask and be honest with Him. Your brutal honesty is not hurting Him. What it is doing is healing you. A lot of times, we are not able to move past our frustration until we have voiced it. I would be careful about going around telling everyone your deepest frustrations with the Almighty, but if you find yourself feeling the need to dress up your frustration or be less than totally honest, don't.

3. *Community*—Some of us may hesitate to honestly share our frustrations with other people, somehow feeling spiritually inferior because we are struggling. It's actually the exact opposite. Those who honestly share their struggles with trusted friends are the spiritually mature. Remember, everyone else struggles too; their struggles just look different. Cultivate a strong Christian group of trusted friends and let them support you when you are weak. You stand a little taller when surrounded by your brothers.

4. *Keep Moving*—There will be times when life is overwhelming. Whether it is emotional, physical, or spiritual difficulty, sometimes it just seems like the storm won't stop. Keep moving. Keep trusting that God is good. Keep investing in your community. Keep your healthy habits. Keep hitting the gym. Keep spending quality time with God. Keep moving, one step at a time. Never quit. If anyone is able to say anything about you, let it be that you keep going no matter what (James 1:12).

DAY 4

Let us throw off everything that hinders and the sin that so easily entangles, and let us run with perseverance the race marked out for us.
HEBREWS 12:1B

HAZARD: FEELING MISUNDERSTOOD

I have often heard this statement from teenage guys: "You don't understand what I'm going through at home. You don't understand my parents. They just don't get it." Instead of parents, it may be a coach or teacher. Maybe it's a friend or acquaintance or a combination of everyone put together. All of us have felt misunderstood at one time or another. It can be extremely frustrating to feel that those around us keep misinterpreting our intentions or simply miss us altogether. As the frustration builds, there are times when we wonder why we even try; it seems that everything we do gets skewed or blown out of proportion. Been there, done that.

Being misunderstood is quite common. The hazard comes when the frustration that results from consistent misunderstanding pushes us into all sorts of destruction. When tempted to act in frustration, we can choose one of three routes. First, we can give in to the frustration and rebel. Our rebellion will look different depending on who, or what, we're rebelling against. In an attempt to spite, we may do the exact opposite of what is expected of us. Some of us stonewall and refuse to communicate with people, while others revert to escalation and end up fighting. We may seek an easy escape from the constant frustration and experiment with drugs or alcohol. When we choose this route, our efforts to spite those who misunderstand us end up damaging us. It reminds me of insurgents who make a bomb intended for someone else and end up accidentally detonating it in their own faces. There is a better way.

Sometimes we are frustrated with people who are trying to help us see we are headed the wrong way. Anytime we encounter misunderstanding, we should take a hard, honest look at ourselves and make any necessary adjustments. Rarely, if ever, are we totally innocent. Maybe we are even the majority of the problem. Most of the time, responsibility for conflict is shared by both parties, requiring both people to adjust and meet in the middle. Don't worry about other people; you can't control them. Focus on what you're responsible for, and then show patience. Remember, we cannot expect others to change if we are not willing to be the change we seek. This is the route we should take most often.

There will be times in your life when you are justified in your action even though people around you are not able to understand. Never was this more true than in Jesus' life. Multiple times in the Gospels, Jesus' family attempted to tame Him, not understanding that God the Father motivated His actions (Mark 3:20-21). The religious establishment of the day definitely misunderstood Him, so much so that they believed He was sent from Satan (Matthew 12:24). Even Jesus' own disciples did not fully understand who He was, hoping they would be given a place of prominence in His kingdom when He threw the Romans out of Jerusalem (Mark 10:35-40). Obviously, the Roman soldiers misunderstood who Jesus was, crucifying Him on a cross. Only one recognized Him after the fact (Matthew 27:54). If anyone had reason to feel misunderstood, it was Jesus, yet we see Him maintain His composure and remain steady, even in the face of death. If you are convicted by the Spirit of God and convinced in your heart to do something, then do it; just don't expect the world to understand (1 Corinthians 2:14). When your cause is right and just, you are called to persevere as Jesus did, disregarding the shame that will come from people far from God (Hebrews 12:2-3). Do not let the frustration that comes from feeling misunderstood drive you to rebellion or keep you from accomplishing what the Lord would have you do.

FORCE MULTIPLIERS

1. *Scripture Memorization*—When we hide God's Word in our hearts, not only are we able to recognize the destruction caused by rebellion but we are able to draw strength from all the misunderstood ones who have gone before us and remained faithful (Hebrews 11:35b-40). Scripture is the tool that convicts us, corrects us, and trains us to know when we should abandon our course, adjust our course, or stay the course. When we fail to spend time in the Word, we severely limit our ability to know which route to take. Stay at it.

2. *Evaluate*—When you feel misunderstood, make sure you carefully evaluate yourself to determine if, or where, you are wrong. This should require you to pull trusted friends into the situation and get another set of eyes to see what you may be missing. Once you've done this, adjust where necessary and own your part of the misunderstanding.

3. *Communicate*—If you want to get to the bottom of the misunderstanding, you must communicate. If you feel misunderstood by a parent, teacher, coach, or friend, go to that person when it is appropriate and honestly share with him or her that you feel misunderstood. Sometimes the issue is legitimate and must be addressed appropriately, but sometimes it is nothing more than your misinterpreting the person's words or actions. You will never know unless you deliberately communicate.

4. *Persevere*—If you are led by God to act, persevere to the end. If or when you are misunderstood, bring in mature Christians who can encourage you and keep you on course. Life is a journey and things typically don't happen overnight, so don't get discouraged. Keep your eyes on Christ and take it a day at a time. Never give up.

DAY 5

Wait for the Lord; be strong and take heart and wait for the Lord.
PSALM 27:14

HAZARD:
INSTANT GRATIFICATION

We live in an instant-gratification culture. We're really quite spoiled. We hear a new song on the radio and are able to identify it by an app that listens to the radio and tells us what song it is. Then we touch a screen and the song is on our phone or computer. If we're hungry, we have food at our disposal almost immediately and we have choices. There's DVR for entertainment and wireless devices for communicating with anyone anywhere in the world, not to mention universal, immediate access to the largest network of information in the history of man. We love our technology, tools that make life easier and offer whatever we want at our fingertips. One of the unintended consequences of the technology surge of the past decade, though, is that we have conditioned ourselves to getting what we want when we want it, making us susceptible to the growing sense of entitlement many people have today. This growing sense of entitlement feeds false expectations and erodes the strength of the church.

A child used to getting his way typically throws a fit when he doesn't. Some things don't change with age; we do the same thing. Our fits are just a bit more mature, but maybe just barely. When most of us want something, we feel entitled to have it immediately. When we don't get what we want, we tend to show our lack of patience by getting irritated or lashing out at someone. Instant gratification stunts our maturity, making us nothing more than grown-up children. We are naïve if we think this does not affect our relationship with God. We sometimes expect the Lord to do whatever we want without delay. Our inability to wait patiently keeps us self-centered, immature Christians, regardless of age. Just because you grow old as a Christian does not mean you've grown up into Christ.

What a lot of us don't realize is that constantly getting what *we* want keeps us from getting what *God* wants for us: the really good stuff. We will always default to the quicker, cheaper option, like someone who ruins his appetite with fast food because he doesn't realize that a choice steak is waiting for him at home. True gratification is always out of reach, with the malnourished desires continuing to demand more and more. C. S. Lewis describes it this way:

> It would seem that our Lord finds our desires not too strong, but too weak. We are half-hearted creatures, fooling about with drink and sex and ambition, when infinite joy is offered us, like an ignorant child who wants to go on making mud pies in a slum because he cannot imagine what is meant by the offer of a holiday at the sea. We are far too easily pleased.[3]

We can either go on playing in the dirt, always reaching but never grasping, or take God at His word and trust that He has something infinitely greater. We must choose. One of the surest signs of growing up into Christ (maturity) is our willingness and ability to delay gratification — to restrain our desire until the right time.

I am certain that everyone reading this today has some sort of unmet desire. You may have aspirations to achieve something great in the academic world, win a championship in athletics, get into a certain school or program, or have your band play in front of thousands. It may be relational; you may wish for your parents to get back together or for that certain girl to notice you. There may be nothing wrong with your desire; just know that the Lord is much more concerned with your personal growth over time than in immediately fulfilling your wishes. God is not in a hurry. He will allow or even bring about difficult situations in our lives to teach us the patience we need to mature in Him.

As we draw near to Him, we may come to see that our desires were misplaced and redirection is necessary. We might realize that an extended period of waiting is exactly what we needed to become the type of people able to handle the things we long for. We are nearsighted; God sees all. Don't sabotage what He is doing in your life because you want a solution right away. You are throwing away the jackpot for chump change.

FORCE MULTIPLIERS

1. *Scripture Memorization*—This is the first line of defense against the lie that true happiness and fulfillment come through instant gratification. In those moments when temptation is most intense, recalling the truth from God's Word will give you the wisdom and insight to recognize and reject the lie. Spiritual maturity starts with daily renewal of the mind.

2. *Fast*—Make it a habit to consistently abstain from something. It may be fasting from food for a day or a week. It may be fasting from media. Turn off the TV and stay away from the computer for a while. Maybe it means turning off your phone for a weekend or longer. Whatever it takes to eliminate distractions and focus on the Lord, do it. This doesn't mean you have to eliminate distractions permanently; maybe start with a fast once every three months or so. This will help you slow down from the fast pace that breeds instant gratification. Be still and listen to the Lord. Focus. Discipline yourself to do this and you will train yourself to keep the perspective and patience needed when life slams you in the face. As C. S. Lewis instructs, "So we must practice in abstaining from pleasures which are not in themselves wicked. If you don't abstain from pleasure, you won't be good when the time comes along. It is purely a matter of practice."[4]

3. *Accountability*—No doubt there are one or more areas of life where

you consistently give in to instant gratification. Maybe it is food or
lust or ambition or something else. Whatever the case, take your
struggle to trusted friends who follow Christ and confess it. Allow
the body of Christ to strengthen and hold you accountable. Owning
your struggle may sting at first, but I think you'll find that your
honesty and willingness to deal with it will begin the healing process
and cultivate the environment necessary for others to deal with their
own selfishness.

AFTER-ACTION
REVIEW

The essence of patience is the choice to pass over what you could have in part now for what will be fully realized in the future. The trouble with many of us today is that we are entirely too shortsighted. Immaturity grasps at only what we can see instead of cultivating the discipline to anticipate a better future. As a result, the instant-gratification culture we live in produces foolish choices that people almost immediately regret. Instead of learning from experience, some individuals typically repeat the same mistake over and over and then take their frustration out on everyone around them. God has called us to something better.

The patient man rejects the temptation to lash out in anger, recognizing that his human anger does not achieve the righteousness God wants for us (James 1:20). He is slow to anger, but in his righteous anger he takes decisive action against injustice and oppression when it is called for. His maturity allows him to recognize his responsibility in conflict. He asks for forgiveness and freely gives it when harmed. When faced with the difficulties of life, his biblical perspective gives him the insight to see his trials as opportunities to grow into a better man instead of becoming indignant toward God. If he is faced with personal injustice, he perseveres, knowing that the Lord will complete His work in His time. Above all, he is not frustrated with his unmet desires, knowing they are only vague hints of something infinitely greater. It has been said, "If I find in myself a desire which no experience in this world can satisfy, the most probable explanation is that I was made for another world."[5]

Far too many young people today vainly grasp for meaning in everything, seeking gratification for their desires in anything they can get their hands on. Show them another way. By your patience, show them that the only thing that will truly meet their desires and satisfy their longing for a better way is found in the person of Jesus Christ.

Here are some questions to help facilitate discussion in your small group. Choose the questions from each day that stick out the most and discuss them as a group. We know it goes without saying at this point, but be open and honest when answering and give grace and mercy to those around you, as you will need the same from them.

Day 1: Anger

1. When is the last time you were angry? What caused your anger? Was there a way to control it?
2. Is there such a thing as righteous anger? If so, explain and back it up with God's Word.
3. Stop, listen, and think are three things we recommended to help control your anger. How can you incorporate these steps into your life?

Day 2: Frustration with Relationships

1. Are you frustrated with a relationship right now? Explain.
2. Have you considered your responsibility for that frustration? What part might you play in the drama?
3. "Low expectations, high flexibility." What does this mean? How can you practice this when dealing with other people?

Day 3: Frustration with God

1. Have you ever been frustrated with God? If so, how?
2. What can we learn from Job about how to handle frustration?
3. What does it look like to keep moving in the midst of your frustration?

Day 4: Feeling Misunderstood

1. What are some ways you feel misunderstood? Why do you think people misunderstand you?

2. When you feel misunderstood, does it push you into rebellion? Why or why not?
3. What are some ways you can communicate to avoid misunderstandings in the future?

Day 5: Instant Gratification

1. Do you consider yourself a patient person?
2. How do you respond when you don't get your way? Do you feel like your response is righteous?
3. Do you ever get tired of waiting on God? Explain.

LOYALTY

DAY 1

A man of many companions may come to ruin, but there is a friend who sticks closer than a brother.
PROVERBS 18:24

HAZARD:
BETRAYAL

It is rare to find a true friend. I'm not talking about surface friendships that don't go any deeper than shared hobbies and time fillers. I'm talking about true friends—people who know you inside and out and stick with you anyway. These are the brothers who fight with you, pray with you, and sacrifice for you.

For many of us, these types of friendships are rare. We are afraid to be vulnerable, especially with another guy. We find it comforting that we have someone to go with to a sporting event or the movies but will stiff-arm anyone who actually tries to get into our lives. Because we are often consumed with our own selfishness, most of us would choose to get ahead or move up the popularity ladder at our friends' expense. We tend to surround ourselves with people who think like we do, and then we are surprised and hurt when those people break promises or double-cross us. It is not enough to ask what type of friends we have; we must ask ourselves what type of friends *we* are.

One of the unsung heroes in the story of David, king of Israel, is his friend Jonathan (1 Samuel 18–2 Samuel 1). Jonathan was the son of the first king of Israel, Saul. He was set to inherit his father's throne; however, his father was disqualified from leadership because of sin, setting up David to become king in Jonathan's place. Jonathan had every reason to be jealous. He could have betrayed his friend, giving lip service to their friendship and, at the same time, going behind David's back to take the crown for himself. Yet he did no such thing. What followed is one of the greatest stories of friendship in the entire Bible. Jonathan consistently looked out for his friend, even placing himself in harm's way to protect David. He selflessly recognized that the Lord chose David to be king and was content to take a backseat to him. Jonathan was eventually killed in a skirmish with the Philistines in northern Israel. When David found out, he wept for his friend: "I grieve for you, Jonathan my brother; you were very dear to me. Your love for me was wonderful, more wonderful than that of women" (2 Samuel 1:26). When brothers truly share life, fight together, reason together, argue together, celebrate together, pray together, a closeness is experienced that can be known only among brothers in Christ. The ones who misunderstand this are the ones who have never experienced this closeness.

What type of friend are you? Are you willing to sell out a friend in order to benefit from it? What if the benefit was a ridiculous amount of money or a social-status upgrade or respect from everyone around you? Is there a price tag on your friendship? Think about it. Are you more willing to bail out of a friendship because you've been burned in the past or do you value your friendships? Do you recognize the worth of true friends and realize there is not a price tag you can place on a true friend? Are you ready and willing at any moment to place your friend above yourself, even if that means putting yourself in harm's way? If it's difficult to honestly answer these questions, take a look at the friends you've decided to surround yourself with—you're probably not that different from them.

There are some people reading this who've never had the honor of experiencing a friendship like David and Jonathan's. Maybe this is the case because of circumstances beyond control, but possibly it is because the necessary time, energy, and selflessness have not been put forth. To have friends like Jonathan, we must *be* friends like Jonathan. Who are you investing in, even when it is not convenient? Who do you honestly share your life with? Who is around when you're vulnerable, when all the armor comes off? Who do you pray with? Who truly knows you? This is a true friend. We pray that if you have such a friend that you will continue to lock arms and journey together toward Christlikeness. If not, we genuinely pray that as you put forth the effort to *be* a true friend, the Lord brings a Jonathan into your life. We stand taller when surrounded by our brothers.

FORCE MULTIPLIERS

1. *Scripture Memorization*—A great way to build up a Christ-centered friendship is to memorize Scripture together. This will hold you accountable to stay disciplined and provide a shared experience that will strengthen your friendship. If you haven't already done so, run this idea by a friend to see if he will join you. Start small with a verse or two (like today's and the others in this book), and then set more challenging goals, such as a section, a chapter, or even a book.
2. *Evaluate*—Take an honest look at how you've wronged a friend, and then go make it right. Others of you have chosen to surround yourself with surface friendships that will never go deeper than mere acquaintances. Some of your acquaintances either already are or will be bad influences. Be honest with yourself and save a lot of trouble and pain. Start to cultivate friendships with people who are serious about following Jesus.
3. *Make Amends*—If you have betrayed someone, whether it was something big or small, go to that person, own your sin, and make amends. None of us is perfect, so don't expect to be, and don't expect others around you to be either. Ask for forgiveness when you are responsible, and give forgiveness when you have been hurt. The ability to do this is crucial for any healthy, lasting friendship.
4. *Be a Jonathan*—Some of you may look at the people around you and have a hard time believing any of them would ever be a true friend. Instead of getting discouraged, be proactive. The best way to have a true friend is to *be* a true friend. Stop sitting around waiting

for a great friend to come along. It doesn't just happen; it takes time, intentionality, and work. Do the things necessary to build a friendship: hang out together, get involved at church together, serve somewhere or lead something together, join the same Bible study, or start a Bible study of your own together.

DAY 2

"Honor your father and mother" — which is the first commandment with a promise — "that it may go well with you and that you may enjoy long life on the earth."

EPHESIANS 6:2-3

 # HAZARD: DISRESPECT

American culture is fiercely individualistic: Our society worships the self. From childhood, we attempt to get our way, doing whatever is necessary to scheme and manipulate situations to our advantage. As we grow, it is natural for us to want to gain a measure of independence from our parents, something that is necessary in order to move away from dependence on them and live as healthy adults. However, independence is not individualism. Too many experience a bit of freedom as teenagers and, instead of maturing slowly into responsibility, bite off more than they can chew. The result is an immature, self-centered rogue who thinks he can do anything he wants, when in reality he hasn't a clue. Because this person does not recognize that the Lord placed others in positions of authority over him for a good reason, he feels suppressed and will go to great lengths to "free" himself from what he sees as threatening to his right to be his own person, even if it costs him his actual freedom.

The primary authority figures during our formative years are our parents. The Lord created it this way because we need it. When left to ourselves, we tend toward chaos. If no one was there to guide and teach us, to correct us when we get off course, we would be left to fend for ourselves with little to no skill in a tough world. Our relationship with our parents is the primary means God has given by which we mature into responsible adults. We may initially view the boundaries placed around us as restrictive, like a child always wanting to climb the playground fence so he can *really* play. What the child doesn't understand is that his lack of maturity and respect for his environment will send him carelessly into the street, where he is met with oncoming traffic. What we may believe to be oppressive is actually in place for our own protection and growth. Rebelling against this authority is self-defeating.

Some of us are naturally more compliant, while others were born with a rebel spirit. Neither is necessarily bad when pointed in the right direction, just different. Regardless of our personalities, whether it comes easy or it is like pulling teeth, we are called to be loyal to our families. Some associate family with comfort and safety and couldn't imagine being disloyal; others cringe at the mention of family. Either way, the call stands to submit to the authority God has placed in your life. We don't respect our parents or authority figures because they deserve it; in fact, some of the time they won't seem to deserve it. We respect them because we love and trust the Lord. There is a direct relation between our respect for God and our willingness to respect the people He has placed in authority over us. Our selfish rebellion against them reflects our disregard for the Lord.

It is interesting that the command to honor your father and mother comes with a promise: "that it may go well with you" (Deuteronomy 5:16). We must respect our parents whether they have earned it or not, not for their sakes but for ours. By learning to submit to authority and respect those roles, we become people who are able to skillfully navigate the turbulent waters of life. This does not mean we will not experience trouble or that everything will suddenly go the way we want; it does mean that whatever life throws at us, whether hardship or success, we can handle it well. When we choose to do it God's way, we become the type of people life agrees with. No one said this would be easy; it is definitely not. There are times when we are so frustrated that rebelling seems to be a very attractive option. Don't do it. Don't short-circuit the maturity process. You're shooting yourself in the foot and showing everyone around you just how little you know.

FORCE MULTIPLIERS

1. *Scripture Memorization*—When our parents or authority figures are overbearing or controlling or just outright mean, choosing to submit can be very difficult. The ability to call to mind Scripture you have committed to memory will give you the wisdom to gain a more accurate perspective on the situation and choose to honor the Lord, despite the chaos around you. Where truth is ignored, lies run wild. Don't become a victim to the lies of the Enemy; the rebellion that makes so much sense at the time will actually destroy your life.

2. *Honor Your Parents*—The Hebrew word for honor is *kavod*. It literally means "heavy." For many, your parents hold practically no weight in your life. You may tend to view your parents as out of touch or incompetent or worse. But consider your position and let's just call it as it is. Your view is based on a lack of life experience. It is to your advantage to show some humility and give your parents weight in your life. Start today. Probably most of us have treated our parents harshly or said extremely hateful things. Go to them and own your disrespect; then ask them for forgiveness. Deny yourself. Admit that you don't have it all figured out. Step up to the role God has called you to. After your parents have picked themselves up off the floor from shock, you may find that relationships can be restored and lives changed.

3. *Forgive and Move On*—Hopefully, honoring your parents will be met with acceptance and love. However, I don't pretend to believe that life is this tidy. Some of your parents don't neatly fit the role that God has designed. We are called to respect anyway. If your parents are lost, whether they claim to be Christian or not, your life may be the best representation of Christ they ever see. Your consistent choice to submit, regardless of whether they deserve it, may be used by God to call them to repentance. Forgive them and move on.

Take responsibility for what God has called you to and leave others up to the Lord. I promise, He is not ignoring them.

For a very few, your parents have forfeited their position of authority in your life. Perhaps they have abandoned or abused you or both. In the case of abuse, go to a different authority for help — for you and your parents. Start with a pastor or trusted friend and go from there. Just as the Lord has called us to honor our parents, He has called parents to protect their children. In abusive situations, the parent is always the one responsible; it is never your fault — ever.

DAY 3

Why do you call me, "Lord, Lord," and do not do what I say?

LUKE 6:46

HAZARD: HABITUAL SIN

Over the years, Brian has watched teenager after teenager slowly drift away from God due to a sin they could never seem to shake. The problem always started small—a passing curiosity—but grew to consume the individual over time. No question, we are all sinners. We are self-serving and proud and jealous and dishonest—on a good day. We will all struggle to varying degrees throughout life, but some of us have been courting a specific sin for so long that it has become habitual. Habitual sin can take any form: a hot temper, compulsive lying, sexual activity, substance abuse, vanity. Whatever the case, this sin, at the very least, stunts our growth and could potentially steal the things we love.

The fact is that all of us have an Achilles' heel, so to speak—a weakness that, if left unchecked, makes us vulnerable to sacrificing our testimony for Christ. The intensity of the struggle may vary depending on the person, but each of us is warring inside. We might feel isolated and unique in our struggle, especially when it is most intense. The apostle Paul described his own struggle with sin in Romans 7:21-24:

> Although I want to do good, evil is right there with me. For in my inner being I delight in God's law; but I see another law at work in me, waging war against the law of my mind and making me a prisoner of the law of sin at work within me. What a wretched man I am! Who will rescue me from this body that is subject to death? (NIV, 2011)

Sound familiar? It definitely sounds familiar to me. So there is literally an unseen battle waging between the Spirit of God inside the ones who believe and the sinful nature we all possess. The question we must answer is Which one will we be loyal to?

There are some who believe we can satisfy both the flesh and the Spirit. They view the grace of God as a license for unrestrained sin. God's grace is always more powerful than sin, so as the severity of sin increases, so does His grace. To stretch this truth as a justification for sin is both irresponsible and evil. Grace does not justify sin any more than seatbelts justify drunk driving. Paul asks in Romans 6:1-2, "Shall we go on sinning so that grace may increase? By no means! We are those who have died to sin; how can we live in it any longer?" (NIV, 2011). No, we are either loyal to our flesh or we are loyal to the Spirit of God. There is no in between or both at the same time. We can't have our cake and eat it too. Claiming loyalty to God and at the same time willingly ignoring His Spirit is so abnormal it prompts Him to ask an appropriate question: "Why do you call me, 'Lord, Lord,' and do not do what I say?" (Luke 6:46). The implication is that we must either start doing what He says or stop calling Him Lord.

Every once in a while, I run across an overly zealous Christian who dreams of doing "great" things for God, even giving his life if needed. There is, of course, nothing wrong with wanting to be used by God in a powerful way, but I often discover that these same people who say they would die for Christ are not willing to live for Him every day. It is a far more significant thing to die to your flesh every day and maintain your loyalty to the Savior.

If habitual sin is trumping your loyalty to God, it is time to die to your flesh once and for all. Men of God call sin what it is and deal with it appropriately. They take their commitment to Christ seriously and meet any threat to their loyalty to Christ with fierceness. As someone who struggles with sin just like everyone else, I know that habitual sin does not simply disappear. We must deal with it openly and allow the Spirit of God to do His cleansing work so that we might rest in

His peace and accurately reflect His character and nature to a lost world.

FORCE MULTIPLIERS

1. *Scripture Memorization*—The temptation to once again give in to habitual sin can be sudden and intense. It's as if you get tunnel vision and have trouble seeing anything other than the desire to gratify the flesh. First Corinthians 10:13 says, "God is faithful; he will not let you be tempted beyond what you can bear. But when you are tempted, he will also provide a way out so that you can endure it" (NIV, 2011). We always have a choice; there is always a way out of temptation. A vast majority of the time, the Scripture you have hidden in your heart is the way out. It's as if a side door breaks into the temptation and you see another way. You must discipline yourself to memorize Scripture consistently. When you stop renewing your mind, that side door out of temptation becomes harder to recognize.

2. *Confess and Repent*—The most effective way to deal with sin aggressively is to confess it. This isn't so tough when you're dealing with sin common to everyone around you; however, when you consistently confess the same sin over and over, it can be frustrating and embarrassing. Don't stop; keep it in the light. Isolation is the other option, and it's a killer. Despite what you might believe, the Lord does not tire of you honestly dealing with your sin, and if your accountability partners are worth their salt, they won't either. If further action is necessary, they will be there to wisely recommend how to get help and then encourage you along the way. Stay connected to the body of Christ, as isolation will destroy your life.

3. *Build Fences*—When you recognize a habitual sin in your life, confess it and drive it away and then build fences to keep it out.

If certain situations tempt you to anger or vanity, stay away from them. If your struggle is substance abuse, you need to switch friends and get into a drug- or alcohol-free environment. If it is pornography, put filters on all your Internet devices. (Do these things anyway.) Be proactive. Take initiative. Building a fence may be the greatest act of loyalty you can do right now.

DAY 4

*Let us not give up meeting together, as some are in the habit of
doing, but let us encourage one another.*

HEBREWS 10:25A

HAZARD:
INCONSISTENCY

There is no doubt you are passionate. You're passionate about extra-
curricular activities, girls, gadgets, and your own time and interests. You
will prioritize your life around these things and spend the most time
and energy on your greatest interest. If you want to know what is most
important to someone, get out his calendar and track his time. He may
give lip service to something, when in reality he spends very little time
in related activities. This gap between intention and practice is unfortunately quite common. Over half of the Christians polled in a survey said
that "they want to have a deep commitment to the Christian faith, but
they are not involved in any intentional effort to grow spiritually."[1] In
other words, most of us would like to call ourselves mature Christians
and probably respect those who are, but we lack the focus, drive, and
commitment it takes to get there. "We have passion, but it is not a
passion for the matters of God."[2]

The fact is that most of us treat the church like a drive-through. We
swing by when it is convenient for us and stay long enough to get what
we want and then we're out. If we are a part of a small group, other
activities or interests typically trump our time with that group. We are
about as consistent as the weather. We put very little effort into spiritual
growth and then wonder why our church seems irrelevant. That makes
about as much sense as failing to put gas in your car and then wondering
why you're stuck on the side of the road. To actually see the results, you
have to put in the time. Not once have I seen a person put the time,

commitment, and work into discipleship and walk away unchanged. Every single time, each committed young man experienced accelerated growth in knowledge, maturity, and intimacy with God. The result was an elevated commitment to the body of Christ: the church. It's funny that the closer you draw to the Lord, the more you gain His heart, a love for the people of God.

Does your schedule accurately reflect the lip service you give your Christian community? Are you consistent with your commitment to your local church? Do you stick with your small group even when something "better" comes up? If not, you need to reevaluate. Either decide to get serious about growing up into Christ or stop pretending you care and go your own way; just don't hang out in the middle. At least be honest. If you are ready to step up and be the man God calls you to be, the first step is to find a mentor — someone a little older, wiser, and further down the road who is willing to walk with you and teach you what it means to be a man of God. You may have to look for a man like this — he's not all that common — but you can start with the youth or young adult pastor at your church. At the very least, get involved with a small group of friends committed to following Christ. (Hopefully, you're already doing this with this book — stick with it.) Lock arms with these guys and put in the time. As a group, decide on a place to serve and then do so. Study God's Word together. Pray together. Stay consistent.

One of my favorite quotes is attributed to a Greek philosopher named Heraclitus on his definition of a true warrior: "For every hundred men you send us, ten should not be here. Eighty are nothing but targets. Nine of them are real fighters; we are lucky to have them, they make the battle. Ah but the one . . . one of them is a warrior, and he will bring the others home."

I know it can be difficult. I know there are times when it seems no one cares. I know the moments of discouragement when you wonder, *What's the point?* Draw strength from our Lord and carry on. You are the one. You are the one who disciplines himself for godliness when no one is looking. You are the one who guards his time with the Lord and truly sees the surpassing greatness of knowing Him. You are the one who puts in the time to make himself a better leader. You are the one others rely on to navigate this life and Enemy territory with skill. You are the one who meets every assault against the body of Christ with accuracy and overwhelming power. You are the one who carries his brothers. You are the warrior. Carry on, brother. Carry on.

FORCE MULTIPLIERS

1. *Scripture Memorization*—As you spend more time with the Lord in His Word, you will gain a new perspective. If you have been consistent with memorizing Scripture to this point in the study, you probably already have a new perspective. You have been taking on the mind of Christ (1 Corinthians 2:16). As we do this, our commitment to His church will increase. The more we take on Scripture, the more the mission of Scripture becomes our mission: to know Christ and make him known.

2. *Get Involved*—Don't just go to church; find a place to get involved. Don't be the guy who simply swings by when it's convenient to take what he wants. Find a place to serve. Be the guy who gives. Find that older guy who's a little further along than you and spend time with him. Ask him to teach you and then commit yourself to learning. If you are older and a bit further along than people around you, spend time mentoring. Give your time and energy to the body of Christ. You will find that what you once thought was irrelevant is actually the most relevant of all.

3. *Make a Difference*—A lot of people spend more time griping about problems in the local church than actually doing anything about them. When you decide to get involved, don't expect a

perfect church—you won't find it. The church is made up of broken people; there will be problems. Instead of griping or looking for a better church, get in there and do something about it. It's amazing what an accurate, focused, consistent effort will produce over time.

DAY 5

He said to them all: "If anyone would come after me, he must deny himself and take up his cross daily and follow me."
LUKE 9:23

HAZARD: MEDIOCRITY

According to J. Oswald Sanders, "Before we can conquer the world, we must first conquer the self."[3] Sadly, too few of us have done this. The landscape of our culture is littered with people who have been conquered by the self. They typically give in to every whim without regard to the consequences or how their actions may affect others around them. Unfortunately, you and I both know this is especially true today. Most people do just enough to get by and squander their God-given potential because they are far more interested in gratifying their own desire, whatever form it takes. We have not led ourselves well. Far too many of us settle for mediocrity and, in so doing, betray the person God wants us to become.

The irony that many of us fail to understand is that the "freedom" we have to indulge the self is actually the very thing that enslaves us. When we do come to realize this, we see that true freedom is found in self-denial, the willingness to shelve our desire for something greater. As we practice this, we get closer to the reality that Jesus spoke of in Caesarea Philippi: "Whoever would save his life will lose it, but whoever loses his life for my sake will find it" (Matthew 16:25, ESV). Denying our selves is not denying our humanity, as some would have you believe; it is the only way to bring the self under control and so realize our humanity in the fullest sense. Our daily prayer should be:

God harden me against myself,
This coward with pathetic voice

Who craves for ease and rest and joys
Myself, arch-traitor to myself;
My hollowest friend, my deadliest foe,
My clog whatever road I go.[4]

To effectively lead ourselves, we must master our desires. When the alarm wakes you to study or exercise or spend time with the Lord, overcome the craving for more sleep and get out of bed. If you have work to do, say no to any distractions that would compromise your priorities, no matter how enticing they are. When any situation gets tough, redouble your efforts instead of giving in to the desire to quit. If we want to reach our full potential in any area of life, we must lead ourselves well. The apostle Paul knew this to be true. He knew that reaching our full potential required a focused plan and strong work ethic: "I do not run like a man running aimlessly; I do not fight like a man beating the air. No, I beat my body and make it my slave so that after I have preached to others, I myself will not be disqualified for the prize" (1 Corinthians 9:26-27). We are all slaves, either to our own desires or to Christ. The men who lead themselves most effectively are the ones chained to Christ.

We will be only as great as the Master we serve. Are we striving after Christ or settling for serving our own selfish desires? In many ways, we can be our own worst enemies. If we settle for less than God's best and are okay with mediocrity, we will never realize just how greatly God can use us. We will never know the joy of success or even the pain of failure. I cannot imagine a worse way for a guy to live his life. It is time to get serious about being loyal to ourselves, to following Christ, to become the men God has called us to be.

FORCE MULTIPLIERS

1. *Scripture Memorization*—The most effective tool we have for mastering the self is God's Word. When we are faced with the temptation to go our own way instead of submitting to the Spirit of God, the truth we have committed to memory illuminates our route and protects us from our own blind spots.

2. *Choose Friends Wisely*—One of the biggest steps in successful self-leadership is carefully choosing the people you hang out with. If you surround yourself with people who push themselves in every area of life, you will be challenged to do the same. Mastering our desires becomes a lot easier when like-minded brothers surround us.

3. *Just Because You Can Doesn't Mean You Should*—Just because everyone else is doing something does not mean you should. Part of self-leadership is determining what is worth doing. Sometimes refraining from an activity allows you to put in the extra work to study or work out or whatever it is that gives you a platform to honor Christ in excellence.

4. *Challenge Yourself*—Get in the habit of doing things that push you. It could be branching out and learning something new or some sort of physical challenge. If you haven't done anything like this in a while, start small with something achievable and work up from there. I think you'll find that your limitations are far fewer than you thought. Get out and do something great. Mediocrity is for the birds.

AFTER-ACTION REVIEW

Loyalty is faithfulness to the principles God says are important. It is being a true friend to a brother in Christ, especially when it is inconvenient or costly. It is recognizing the authority structure the Lord created for your good and respecting it. You are loyal when you recognize your own depravity and do the hard work to overcome the sin that would betray the Savior. It is rejecting "drive-through" Christianity and diligently serving the body of Christ where you are needed. Loyalty is embracing self-leadership and fully realizing your potential to be a change agent for Christ to the people around you. Men of God are absolutely loyal to the Lord, their family, their friends, their church, and their potential.

In a world that embraces self-gratification, finding a truly loyal person is becoming more and more difficult. As teenagers and young adults, your loyalties are being pulled from all sides by a turbulent culture. You face difficult decisions every day that tempt you to place your own selfish desire above your loyalty to others. It is key to be aware of whatever would steal your devotion to being the man God has called you to be. Understand your environment and the hazards that exist within it. The choice to remain faithful is not made in the moment; it is decided before you are ever in a compromising situation. If you fail to work through the damaging implications of betrayal prior to temptation, you will tend to choose self-preservation and self-gratification over loyalty. Too many have already walked this path.

God is not asking you to do something He hasn't done already. We will never fully understand Jesus' being tempted in the desert by the Enemy. The entire temptation boiled down to Jesus' keeping all the power without following God and redeeming you and me through the Cross. I'm sure that Jesus' natural self-preservation triggers were firing as a man, knowing that immeasurable suffering lay ahead, yet He had the vision to see past the Enemy's offer that wasn't his to give. Jesus kept His eye on what truly mattered: faithfulness to His Father and, in turn, the redemption of the whole world. He maintained His loyalty and calls you to do the same.

Reject self-serving actions and maintain your loyalty because the One who has your best interests in mind tells you to. As you trust Him and remain faithful to His call on your life, He makes you look like His Son, and like His Son, you may one day hear, "Well done, good and faithful servant!" (Matthew 25:21).

Here are some questions to help facilitate discussion in your small group. Choose the questions from each day that stick out the most and discuss them as a group. You know the drill: be open and honest when answering and give grace and mercy to those around you, as you will need the same from them.

Day 1: Betrayal

1. Have you or has anyone close to you been betrayed? What was the response?
2. What did you learn about loyalty from Jonathan?
3. Do you consider yourself a loyal friend? What does loyalty mean to you?

Day 2: Disrespect

1. Why do you think it is so hard to respect authority?
2. How does it make you feel when someone disrespects you?
3. How hard is it to forgive and move on? What helps you do this?

Day 3: Habitual Sin

1. What sins came to mind as you read day 3? (Be honest — you know what came to mind.)

2. Why do you think it is so hard to turn away from sin and give it to God? What keeps us from repentance?

3. "There is nothing wrong with wanting to be used by God in a powerful way, but I often discover that these same people who say they would die for Christ are not willing to live for Him every day." Do you find that to be true? Give some examples of how you can take up your cross daily, dying to self and following Christ.

Day 4: Inconsistency

1. How does inconsistency damage your walk with God? How does it affect other people's view of Christianity?

2. What are some practical steps you can take to get involved on a regular basis?

3. Does the time you spend accurately reflect the lip service you give your Christian community? If not, why?

Day 5: Mediocrity

1. "Before we can conquer the world, we must first conquer the self." Do you believe this is true? What does it mean for you?

2. Do you ever not finish what you start? What keeps you from finishing?

3. "Just because you can doesn't mean you should." What is the daily application of this statement? In what ways are you set apart from your lost friends?

ENTHUSIASM

DAY 1

The way of the sluggard is blocked with thorns, but the path of the upright is a highway.
PROVERBS 15:19

HAZARD: APATHY

The teenage and young-adult years are some of the most exciting times of life. The youthful enthusiasm of high school and college students is contagious. It is a rare thing, however, to find focused, meaningful enthusiasm. Most of it is unbridled excitement that has little to do with anything, except maybe girls, school spirit, or just having a good time. The trouble is not that youth aren't enthusiastic, it's that the other side, apathy, shows up in the areas of life that matter most. Have you ever lost interest in something because it was too hard? Do you find it difficult to take risks? Have you ever stopped caring about a goal because, for whatever reason, you can't quite seem to reach it? Probably all of us can identify with at least one of these signs of apathy.

Apathy, a general attitude of not caring, or indifference, occurs for a number of reasons, but two consistently stand out. First, we are self-absorbed. Instead of keeping a broader perspective of the world and the other people in it, we tend to see ourselves and our circumstances at the moment. When we are slaves to the self, we grasp at whatever feels good at the moment. Because we do this consistently over time, habits are formed. Because habits are formed, anything that requires hard work or dedication to achieve something greater than the self is typically abandoned. We quit. We fail to step up and face challenges. We say such things as "I don't care" and "Whatever" a lot. We become apathetic, happy to merely exist and get whatever fleeting pleasure we can out of life. As sinful people prone to wander from the Lord, this is quite common.

Sadly, the result of this attitude is also common. A lot of us miss out on the opportunity to shape and form a strong character because we quit when things get tough or don't go our way. Instead of working hard to get a good education, many students sacrifice a better future for a few years of partying or easy answers. We only cheat ourselves in the end. An enormous potential for good is squandered due to apathy. We spend unreasonable amounts of time and energy on things that ultimately do not matter, sometimes on things that destroy us, while we display a general attitude of indifference toward the areas of life that shape us into men of God. No wonder there are so few godly men today.

The second reason apathy exists is because very few people have a clear vision of what they want out of life. Even fewer actually set goals and work at them to achieve their dream. Most are just wandering around in the dark, always dreaming but never learning to cultivate vision. Unfortunately, many teenagers and young adults have never been taught how to take a dream and make it into a realistic, achievable goal. More often than not, attempts to fulfill a dream are misguided and ultimately fall short. It is all too easy to drift into apathy after we have tried again and again to make our vision a reality, only to be met with disappointment.

Vision is the capacity to picture a desired future, but unless we narrow our focus and prayerfully consider what steps will lead us toward our dream, vision is rarely realized. A vision without a goal is just a good idea. We need men of vision, but we need men motivated enough to implement the vision and make it a reality. Reed and Hunter, seniors in high school, are great examples of men like this. They identified a need on their football team for spiritual leadership, so they decided it would be a good idea to step up and bring in area youth pastors to speak to the entire team every Thursday at 3 p.m. Instead of simply recognizing a good idea, they worked to make it happen. The guys organized the meetings and scheduled a speaker for each week. At the time we wrote this book, 60 percent of their public-school football team now goes to church. That number will probably increase, thanks to their vision.

These guys had a picture of a desired future and—armed with an accurate, achievable plan—they worked to accomplish it. Look around you and ask God to give you His vision. How can you positively impact the people around you? What are some practical steps you can take to make the vision the Lord has given you a reality? Share your ideas with a friend and take small, achievable steps toward your goal. I think you'll find that any attitudes of indifference will fade away. You only live once, so don't waste an opportunity.

FORCE MULTIPLIERS

1. *Scripture Memorization*—It's tough to take in doses of God's Word every day and stay apathetic. Scripture motivates. It helps narrow your focus. It gives you insight, which turns into the foresight that, when properly implemented, changes the world around you.
2. *Evaluate*—Do you spend most of your time and effort on things that have no lasting value? Are you more interested in living for yourself than sacrificing for others? Take an honest look at your life. Do you quit easily? Are you showing signs of apathy and indifference? Recognizing and owning your apathy is the first step to living a fulfilled, enthusiastic life.
3. *Be Specific*—Most of the time, people dream much too broadly. You may have a very general picture of who you want to be, but without narrowing the vision, it will always stay a dream. Once you have a desired picture of the future, work back from that image and determine what steps need to be taken to get there. Start small with the basics and work up from there. If the initial steps you take are specific enough to be measurable, you will be encouraged as you consistently meet your goals. Before you know it, what was once a thought will be a reality.

4. *Pray with Your Friends*—You may not have any idea how your future is supposed to look. It's okay; your vision is a clean slate. Go to the Lord and ask Him what He wants for you. I promise you that if you share with your small group your desire to make an impact among your peers and then consistently pray for it, God will clarify the vision in your mind. If you pray consistently with your friends, the vision may become so clear in your mind that it will seem impossible for it not to become a reality.

DAY 2

*Do nothing out of selfish ambition or vain conceit, but in humility
consider others better than yourselves. Each of you should look not
only to your own interests, but also to the interests of others.*

PHILIPPIANS 2:3-4

HAZARD:
SELF-CENTEREDNESS

Have you ever noticed that the times we are down or experience the
most frustration or anger all share one common denominator? We are
focused on ourselves. We lose our joy because we dwell on a problem or
issue we're experiencing at the moment. We are frustrated because someone has ruined our plans, or we are angry because we feel that life has
thrown a wrench into our ambition. Maybe someone else is enjoying the
success you have been working for. Regardless, we all have a serious
problem: We tend to center an inordinate amount of attention on the
self. Scripture calls this demonic and the source of "disorder and every
evil practice" (James 3:14-16). Self-centeredness is the surest way to rob
your enthusiasm.

For the most part, self-centeredness manifests itself in three different
ways. Some of us are just straight-up vain. We spend a lot of time flexing
in the mirror and talking trash about ourselves. The deception is in
thinking that purpose and meaning can be found by feeding ourselves an
almost constant diet of the self. We then become fattened with pride and
struggle to find meaning anywhere. But at least the guy with a massively
swollen ego is obvious. He typically clashes with other people—people
the Lord may use to humble him.

A much less obvious self-centeredness is a negative obsession with
self. Those of us who tend toward this have just as big an ego as the first
guy, but it just happens to be a negative focus. We will complain about

almost everything. We tend to blame everyone else for our problems and spend too much time moping about. In serious cases, this type of focus on self drives us to depression. No question that by focusing on the self, we are attempting to remedy our pain; however, in doing so, we dig ourselves further into a hole. We give ourselves way too much credit. Basically, if you want to live a miserable life, focus on yourself all the time.

Finally, the most dangerous self-centeredness is the kind couched in spiritual piety. The authors of *Overcoming the Dark Side of Leadership* wrote, "As human beings we have an inherent ability to deceive ourselves. Thus equipped we are capable of transforming even the most selfishly motivated action into an act of sacrificial altruism in our own minds."[1] Selfishness is so deeply ingrained in us that it will disguise itself as "service" or "using our gifts," when in reality, the sole purpose behind our action is the vain desire to get ahead or elevate our standing in the eyes of those around us. Our actions are not necessarily wrong, but our motives could not be more evil. We should follow David's example and ask the Lord to search our hearts and convict us of any tendencies to idolize ourselves (Psalm 139:23-24). As long as we are fooling ourselves, we will never know the great enthusiasm that comes from following the Lord with a pure heart.

At the risk of sounding too dramatic, when it comes to our tendency to give the self more attention than it can handle, we really ought to kill our selfishness. There is nothing wrong with our desires; God gave them to us. However, they are meant to be ruled, not to rule over us. When controlled by our selfishness, they wreak all kinds of havoc. Nothing good ever comes from self-centeredness. On the other hand, those who learn to turn their focus away from the self and give their desires over to the lordship of Jesus Christ experience the enthusiasm of life in the fullest sense. Interesting that the very One who created us with the capacity to know great joy and fulfillment "did not come to be served, but to serve, and to give his life as a ransom for many" (Mark 10:45). It seems to make sense that we should follow the example of the Creator.

Take the focus off yourself and put it on other people. You'll find your enthusiasm for life exploding with new energy.

FORCE MULTIPLIERS

1. *Scripture Memorization*—Nothing is more lethal to selfishness than God's truth that stands directly against it. Taking in daily doses from God's Word will help you guard against taking in daily doses of the self. It keeps us sharp against overt self-centeredness and the deceitful kind as well. Scripture is the only thing able to judge "the thoughts and attitudes of the heart" (Hebrews 4:12).

2. *Serve*—You cannot think about two things at once: Either you are thinking about yourself or something related to the self, or you are thinking about others. One of the most practical ways to train yourself to have an "others focused" perspective is to serve. Find a place at church or in the community that interests you and get involved. Check your motives to make sure they're pure, and then go spend yourself on other people. It's what Jesus did.

3. *Encourage*—Encouragement is literally speaking life into someone. Some of the most meaningful times in my life were spent in "strength rallies" encouraging other men. Nathan's dad gave this name to intentional times of encouragement. Focusing on a person's positive attributes and naming them out loud makes an immeasurable difference. Something interesting happens every time you encourage someone. It strengthens the individual and infuses enthusiasm into you. Nothing is more contagious.

Am I now trying to win the approval of men, or of God? Or am I trying to please men? If I were still trying to please men, I would not be a servant of Christ.

GALATIANS 1:10

HAZARD: INSECURITY

Have you ever been weighed down because you felt inadequate around other people? Are you more concerned with other people's opinions than about living life to the fullest? It is extremely common for young guys to be preoccupied with attempting to measure up to some undefined standard of manhood. Typically, this involves simply trying to be like the other guys in a group. What is meant to be a season of discovery and enthusiasm can end up being totally awkward. Many times our insecurities keep us from stretching our legs and enjoying life. Our development not only as men but also as Christians will be stunted as long as we are consumed with what other people think about us.

We see a lot of teenagers who go to great lengths trying not to stand out as being different. The amount of effort they put into this ends up sucking the joy out of life. It is exhausting always trying to be someone you're not. What most of these students fail to realize is that everyone is different because God created us that way. He made us each with our own fingerprint, with intricacies that should be embraced and celebrated, not altered to imitate the next guy. We should appreciate our differences and learn to laugh at our quirks. While insecure people tend to make everyone around them nervous, there is something liberating about a person who just isn't worried about what other people think.

I once had to spend some time around a very insecure individual. Without saying so, he made it very clear that he wanted to be well thought of by everyone, but by projecting his lack of confidence, he alienated the very people he cared so much to please. His life was almost totally lacking in any kind of real enthusiasm. He consistently used a negative tone and was always complaining about something, yet he very much wanted to be viewed as a leader. His insecurity was self-defeating.

I also had the privilege of growing up with a very different type of person. He was secure in who God made him, quirks and all. Instead of trying to adjust to fit in with everyone else, he celebrated his differences and blazed his own trail. He could not have cared less what other people thought about him and instead displayed an authenticity that was contagious. People were naturally drawn to him and appreciated his differences. His demeanor allowed everyone around him to relax and be themselves, cultivating an environment of growth. He has been consistently marked by enthusiasm for life, and people are better having known him.

Which guy does your life most resemble? Do you care too much about the opinions of others, or do you recognize that God created you as you are for good reason? Is it more important for you to be well respected for being someone you aren't or for you to be authentic regardless of what people think? Is your life characterized by true enthusiasm, or are you just playing games? There's only one of you, so be yourself. The Lord created you to be just the way you are.

FORCE MULTIPLIERS

1. *Scripture Memorization*—The world will tell you to conform to a standard that is always changing. Trying to fit into our society is like chasing the wind. What's in one day is out the next and vice versa. A lot of time and money is wasted by people simply trying to keep up. Scripture says that we are "fearfully and wonderfully made"

(Psalm 139:14). Hide God's Word in your heart and allow it to influence your life.

2. *Be Yourself*—Relax and be yourself. If people don't like you for who you are, it's okay; not everyone has to like you. Plenty of people will accept you for who you are, and they are the ones who matter. Use your unique personality and gifts to serve the body of Christ and further the kingdom. Enthusiasm is cultivated and matures as we live for Christ, not other people.

3. *Learn to Laugh*—Everyone has his quirks. Don't be embarrassed by the things that make you unique. Learn to laugh at them. We aren't telling you to totally disregard everyone around you and act a fool; we are encouraging you to be comfortable enough in your own skin to appreciate the things that make you a little weird. By creating each of us different, God made us all the same.

DAY 4

Remember the Sabbath day by keeping it holy.
EXODUS 20:8

HAZARD: BURNOUT

Stress can be our best friend or worst enemy. Positive stress is the normal pressure that pushes us to succeed. It guards against atrophy and apathy. The right amount of stress feeds our passion and drives us to achieve great things. For all of us, especially the gifted overachiever, though, there is an underlying danger of overextending ourselves and our ability to maintain a healthy workload. When the load we carry outweighs our capacity, we are in danger of burning out. Depending on the amount of stress, our passions either consume us or destroy us.

Burnout can occur in any area of life, but it is particularly dangerous for Christians. Our desire to do great things for God is often coupled with our insecure need for approval and the false expectations we project on ourselves. The symptoms of burnout frequently go undetected because they are dressed up with great achievement for God. Because our achievement is met with self-fulfillment and applause, we continue to overextend ourselves out of a desire for more gratification and praise, working at a tempo that is not sustainable. As said by the authors of *Overcoming the Dark Side of Leadership*, "We can run at a frantic pace, driven by the expectations of others and ourselves, for only so long before we freeze up and spin dangerously out of control."[2]

Sometimes the symptoms of burnout come gradually, and sometimes they hit us like a load of bricks. The first sign of burnout is withdrawal. We might place our faith in Christ and initially be filled with such enthusiasm that we would readily charge the gates of hell with a water pistol. We willingly volunteer to serve the church in multiple capacities and are entrusted with more responsibility as we prove ourselves faithful. The danger of carrying more than we can handle has already begun. If we are gifted and willing to serve, most churches will run us into the ground if we let them. Sooner or later, we start losing steam and gradually distance ourselves from the church. What once ignited a passion in our hearts now seems to weigh us down. If we fail to slow down, our attitude toward the church can become critical and bitter, making it easier to blame God for something we've brought on ourselves.

When we begin to experience the first signs of burnout, those of us who are really driven will push through it, seeing it more as an obstacle than a signal to slow down. If we continue to push it, the next mark of burnout is physical and emotional exhaustion. Our bodies can take only so much stress. If our misplaced ambition causes us to pour on more and more, our minds and bodies will eventually start to shut down. Physical health problems may start to surface; stress will make our bodies do some crazy stuff. If we continue to ignore the warnings and press on through the exhaustion, we will drive ourselves to depression and despair. At this point, we are completely burned out. In most cases of burnout, people experience a measure of doubt, questioning everything from personal competence to faith to God Himself. What was once a rock-solid foundation seems to fall apart. The same enthusiasm that drove us to achieve is the very thing that will burn us out if we're not careful.

Some of you reading this are too young to fully understand burnout. Many of you have probably experienced at least the first signs of burn-out. More than likely, there are a few who are either getting close to total burnout or are already there. Regardless, pay attention. It is much better to seek help earlier than later. If you are experiencing any level of burn-out, slow down and seek counsel from someone who's been there. Be careful who you talk to; some people will tell you to keep exhausting yourself, couching it in spiritual-sounding language such as "You just need to persevere" or "Just keep believing." There is a difference between persevering in faith and taking a nosedive into the ground. One of the most spiritual things we can do is rest. Some of you are so wound up that you don't even know how to kick back and relax.

Life, especially the Christian life, is not a sprint; it's a marathon. Plenty of people have driven themselves into the ground, attempting to accomplish what they believe that God wants them to do, but no one ever made a lasting impression on the world for Christ this way. We have to get away from the emphasis we place on achieving great things for God and start emphasizing the greatness of simply knowing Him. He is infinitely more interested in what type of person you are than what types of things you do. Learning that purpose and fulfillment come only through our relationship with Christ and not our accomplishment is the first step to freeing ourselves from the need to gain approval, affirmation, and the burnout that is sure to follow.

FORCE MULTIPLIERS

1. *Scripture Memorization*—"We must realize that consistent exposure to Scripture will provide us with the most accurate self-knowledge available to us."[3] The key to avoiding burnout is to have an accurate understanding of ourselves. In a world full of different voices telling us who we should be, Scripture is the only absolute voice we should trust. The more Christlike our thoughts, the quicker we will be able to recognize the warning signs of burnout and make necessary adjustments. We must continue to renew our minds daily with God's Word.

2. *Learn to Say No*—If someone is talented and driven, more and more opportunities will present themselves. If you find yourself here, you have to move beyond ambition and people pleasing and realize that sometimes the healthiest thing to do is say "no" or "not now," especially if you have already noticed signs of burnout. This can be a difficult thing to do, particularly if the opportunities are important.

Keeping a long-term perspective will allow you to see that the kingdom of God will continue to move forward even if you are not the one out front. In fact, that may be the very thing you need to learn.

3. *Rest*—Resting does not necessarily mean taking a vacation. Sometimes vacations are so busy that we need a vacation from our vacation. Resting is intentional time set aside when everything is turned off and you are able to relax. It could include spending time with people you love or spending extended quality time with the Lord. Regardless, to maintain our enthusiasm, all of us need to learn to recharge our batteries and ultimately find that power in Christ.

DAY 5

My flesh and my heart may fail, but God is the strength of my heart and my portion forever.

PSALM 73:26

HAZARD:
DEPRESSION

Depression continues to be a difficult subject, despite the fact that it is discussed openly today. Addressing it requires people to be extremely vulnerable and honest about the deepest parts of their lives. It is not easy, but it must be dealt with because it is a very real part of life for people of all ages.

Suicide is the third leading cause of death among teenagers, almost always a result of depression.[4] By age eighteen, some 20 percent of adolescents have experienced at least one episode of serious depression.[5] That's one out of every five. Estimates show that, among teenagers, for every suicide, there are fifty to two hundred suicide attempts.[6] There is no doubt that depression is a serious problem today. Many people have a misplaced belief, bordering on arrogance, that depression is something that happens to "weak" people. Some have failed to recognize that symptoms of depression are already present in their lives. A few don't see it at all until they slam into the wall. Nathan slammed into one such wall. This is his story:

I was coming to the end of my master's degree program at Dallas Theological Seminary (DTS) in the fall of 2005. To say I was busy is an understatement. I believed that because I had the capacity to juggle work, school, and multiple ministry roles, I should do so, thinking that anything less meant I was not fully utilizing the gifts God had given me for His kingdom. If pushed, I probably would have admitted that I was pursuing approval from God by doing so much; after all, I had grown up an athlete who connected performance with pats on the back and the roar of the crowd. I was relying on *my* strength to achieve what *I* could for God. My theology was orthodox; my practice was not.

After ignoring clear warning signs, I began to hit the wall. I noticed that I was losing my ability to control my thoughts. My mind would fixate on something, usually something strange, and then once it latched onto a thought, no matter how hard I tried I could not stop thinking about it. In fact, the harder I tried to fight against it, the worse it got. For someone who loved a sense of control, I felt very powerless. I was convinced I was going nuts. The irrational thoughts brought with them an enormous amount of fear and anxiety, and I started to lose sleep. My brain never turned off. My muscles were always tense and would twitch from stress. My defenses were down and I was completely vulnerable to the lies of the Enemy. Even though I could tell you what was true, I did not feel like it was. At my lowest point, I gave all my personal weapons to a friend because I was afraid I would harm myself. After I finally got to sleep that night, I woke up in a panic and, heart racing, crawled to the bathroom and threw up in the toilet. I could not sleep. I could not work. I was barely finishing my assignments. I was totally out of control.

I was very fortunate to be in an environment that did not stigmatize depression. After meeting with a counselor, he referred me to a doctor in town who started me on low doses of an antidepressant. I continued to meet with the counselor, who helped me identify some of the core issues I was dealing with. I was completely honest with my trusted friends, who provided the encouragement and support necessary for me to heal properly. I started eating right and exercising on a regular basis. Approximately six to eight weeks later, I noticed a marked difference. I was sleeping again. My thoughts were not running wild. I was no longer robbed of my joy. After three months of a focused, holistic approach to recovery, I felt completely normal. I had experienced God's grace in a whole new way.

There are three major lessons the Lord taught me through this experience. First, empathy. Before this experience, I honestly wondered why some people couldn't just suck it up and drive on. Now, having been in those shoes, I am able to empathize with those who struggle with depression, to come alongside people and weep with them (Romans 12:15). Then, when the time is right, I gently share the steps I took to recover and encourage them to make wise decisions, whether they feel like it or not.

Which leads to the second lesson: Scripture is the only anchor in the midst of a raging storm. If something is true, it is true regardless of how you feel about it. In my darkest times, I still made it a point to get into God's Word, even though I struggled to believe it. I was consistently faced with the choice to either take God at His word or give in to fleeting emotions or powerful lies from the Enemy. Because I surrounded myself with strong believers, I was reminded on a regular basis of the truth. Over time, I came to know an intimacy in my walk with Christ I had never known. One of the greatest gifts the Lord has ever given us is His written word. It is the compass that will lead us home.

Third, I learned that we are holistic people. We are complex creatures made up of many different pieces. We are physical beings with bodies susceptible to dysfunction. We are spiritual, with an ongoing battle between the Spirit of God and our self, the part of us that will, if we allow it, naturally drag us into depression. I learned that there is not a simple fix for a complex person. Complex problems require complex solutions. If a man is to recover from depression, he must address every part of his person: mind, body, and spirit.

Some of you have dealt with depression in the past; some of you are struggling through it right now. Words like enthusiasm, joy, and peace have lost meaning. You may have identified with parts of my story or maybe the whole thing. Whatever the case, take heart: The Lord will not leave you where you are. If you allow Him to, He will bring clarity into your life and use an extremely difficult time to give you a depth you would not have known otherwise. Put the following force multipliers into practice and never lose hope. There is always hope.

FORCE MULTIPLIERS

1. *Scripture Memorization* — This is absolutely essential when dealing with depression. Once in a depressed state, all rationality can fly out the window. You are wide open to attacks from the Enemy. Knowing and choosing to believe the truth in these times is key to avoiding lasting damage. You always have a choice. There is no other way. God's Word is the only solid thing in a weak state.

2. *Exercise* — If you struggle with depression, you *have* to exercise. When you exercise, chemicals called endorphins are released in your brain. These are the body's natural response to depression. If your brain is an engine, endorphins are the oil that helps it run properly. Along with a properly balanced diet (eat fish or take a fish oil supplement), exercise is the most practical physical step you can take toward recovery.

3. *Community* — Depressed people are faced with two options: be proactive and get help, or isolate and continue to spiral out of control. You are already exposed to the Enemy's lies; isolation only makes this worse. In extreme cases, someone who remains isolated can ultimately believe the lie that there is no hope, causing him to take his life. Isolation can be lethal. Community provides the strength you need to stand. True friends will listen to you, encourage you, and walk with you in the darkness. They are an essential part of coming out of depression.

4. *Walk by Faith* — "We must live according to truth, not feelings. . . . Even in times of defeat or frustration or failure, as we walk by faith not by sight, we can know that we are valuable because of our standing with God in heaven."[7] Faith is choosing to hope when it seems hopeless.

5. *Focus on Others* — At its heart, depression is an obsession with self. Realizing this is a key step to recovery. You must make a

concentrated effort to focus on others. Once the Lord showed me this, I kept an index card with me (this was before smartphones) and consistently asked others how I could pray for them. Then I would pray for them. It's amazing how little we think of our own issues when we are focused on other people.

6. *Seek Professional Help* — If you actively implement these force multipliers, most of you will come out of your depression. However, some of you have slipped into a deep depression that requires further attention. As I mentioned in my story, complex problems require complex solutions. If you need medication or structured counseling by a professional to start you on the road to recovery, get the help. There is nothing unspiritual about this. It can be a life-changing step of faith.

AFTER-ACTION
REVIEW

The summer between Eric's junior and senior years in high school, he went to a summer camp with his church. During the course of that week, he was challenged, along with some friends, to spend his senior year using the influence God had given him to make an impact for the Lord on his school campus. He didn't know exactly what he was supposed to do or how all that was going to play out, but he just had a deep conviction that he needed to get his friends together to pray. Although they appreciated the See You at the Pole movement that encouraged students across the country to come together each year on the fourth Wednesday in September to pray for their school, they wondered why something like this happened only once a year. So they started praying at the school flagpole every day. They didn't pray long—just long enough to lift up a handful of requests and pray for God's favor on the campus. But they prayed. They prayed in the heat. They prayed in the cold. They even prayed in the rain. Initially there were only a handful of people consistently praying, but the group grew over time. Before they knew it, the group exploded in number.

The prayer group was consistent but also strategic. The Lord had called the most influential students on campus to pray: the captain of the football team, the captain of the men's basketball team, the captain of the women's basketball team, the worship leader at a local church. Because of the broad influence present, the entire campus took notice of what was going on. To support the group, a local church held an evangelistic youth rally where many students from the school placed their faith in Christ. It was unmistakable that the Spirit of God was moving on campus, all because God put it in the hearts of a couple of students to pray.

Because Eric was one of the captains of the basketball team, he sometimes spoke at school pep rallies. Before one such rally, he approached an accountability partner and told him that he felt the Lord calling him to share the gospel. His friend basically told him that if God was telling him to do something, he'd better do it. So he did. In front of about two thousand peers, he unashamedly told of sin, grace, and the saving work of Christ on the Cross. What started the prior summer as a thought in his head turned into having the entire school hear the gospel of Jesus Christ. One young man full of enthusiasm made himself available to be used by God for that time and place. In the grand scheme of things, making a difference on that campus was a small splash in a big pond, but that splash rippled out into eternity.

Enthusiasm is a combination of two Greek words that literally mean "in God." To experience enthusiasm in its truest sense, we must tap into the joy and passion that comes from walking intimately with our Creator. The world is in desperate need of young men of God who reject apathy, self-centeredness, and insecurity. We have way too many of those already. Be different. Swim against the stream. Live a life that invests in eternity. Serve others. Stand apart. Do outstanding things. God wants to use you in a powerful way. Let Him. When you experience the joy that comes from living a life firmly rooted in Christ, you will wonder why you ever thought anything else would fulfill you. How will your school be different because you were there? Be an Eric. Be a light in the darkness. The Lord will set you on fire and people will come for miles to watch you burn.[8]

Here are some questions to help facilitate discussion in your small group. Choose the questions from each day that stick out the most and discuss them as a group. This is the final week in this book, so keep being open and honest when answering and give grace and mercy to those around you, as you will need the same from them.

Day 1: Apathy

1. Do you think the "I don't care" attitude is a problem? How?
2. What harm does it do when we quit what we started? Is there ever a right time to quit?
3. What does a motivated man of vision look like?

Day 2: Self-Centeredness

1. Out of the three examples we gave (vanity, negative self-obsession, and spiritual piety), which one do you think you struggle with the most?
2. How can you humble yourself and serve someone this week? When is the last time you inconvenienced yourself to help someone else?
3. List five characteristics of a selfless person.

Day 3: Insecurity

1. How do you define the word *insecurity*?
2. Do you find it difficult to just be yourself? Either way, why? Do you think others find it difficult? Why?
3. What does the force multiplier "Learn to laugh" mean to you?

Day 4: Burnout

1. Do you have a hard time saying no to stuff? What do you think is behind your driven personality?
2. What are some warning signs of burnout? Do you see any of these in your life? If so, what steps will you take to rest and protect yourself against burnout (or even depression)?
3. How is resting in Christ different from taking a vacation? Is this something you can do every day?

Day 5: Depression

1. How common is depression among your peers? How have you been down or depressed?

2. Do you feel you have a quality group of friends you can go to at anytime?

3. What are steps you should take to recover from depression?

WRAP-UP

1. What is the most significant truth you learned during your time in this book and in God's Word?

2. How has the Spirit been at work transforming you? What changes have occurred?

3. Have you experienced specific victories by identifying hazards and utilizing the force multipliers in this book?

4. Who needs to know the checkpoints, hazards, and force multipliers you are now practicing? Part of maturing and becoming a godly man is helping others also grow up into Christ (Ephesians 4:11-16), so who will you now invite to walk through these biblical life principles?

CLOSING

As long as we have breath, there is no finish line to manhood. You don't graduate from it or win it like a championship. There's no diploma to hang or trophy to display. It is a lifelong journey of consistently disciplining yourself to conform to the standard set forth in Scripture. No one expects you to do this perfectly, least of all God, who knows you better than you know yourself. I was recently reminded of this fact on a road trip with one of my accountability partners. We caught up with each other and then shared our struggles and owned our sin, two principles emphasized in this study. The need for growth in our lives was evident to both of us, stark reminders that we have not yet arrived.

Honestly, I am sometimes frustrated by the process the Lord has chosen for maturing us. It is a messy process, marked by success and failure. As you walk this journey, you will realize it is accurate to say that some areas of your life are more Christlike and mature while other areas need more work, sometimes a lot of work. I think C. S. Lewis nailed it when he was asked, "Will you please say how you would define a practicing Christian? Are there any other varieties?" He answered,

> Certainly there are a great many other varieties. It depends, of course, on what you mean by "practicing Christian." If you mean one who has practiced Christianity in every respect at every moment of his life, then there is only one on record — Christ himself. In that sense there are no practicing Christians, but only Christians who, in varying degrees, try to practice it and fail in varying degrees and then start again.[1]

Though the road is marked by struggle, we must never get complacent or settle for less than the Lord's standard. Maturity is not earned; it is practiced. Discipline yourself in the basic fundamentals and you will find an identity grounded in Christ. You will become a man of integrity who, through the power of the Holy Spirit and in authentic Christian community, learns to control the self. The courage, patience, loyalty, and enthusiasm will naturally follow.

Each individual is unique. There is no way we can cover all of the many different facets of manhood for every single person. Our task has been to lay out biblical principles and the practical steps that follow to tactically guide you through the process of maturing. This brings us to one of the most dangerous hazards of all: discipline as an end unto itself, not the means to something (or someone) greater. What I mean is that you go about implementing the force multipliers given in this book but lose sight of the actual power that makes you a man. It's like having all the parts assembled and ready to roll but no fuel in the tank. In the end, true manhood is not earned by what you do but rather gained by the transformation that comes through who you know.

A certain Jewish man who walked the hills of Palestine roughly two thousand years ago claimed some extraordinary things about Himself. It would have been easy to dismiss Him were it not for the things He did. He said He was the bread of life, and He also fed a crowd of people with one kid's lunch. He said He was the resurrection and life, right before He told a dead guy to get up—and he did. He claimed to be the Son of God but was declared so with power by the resurrection from the dead (Romans 1:4). Jesus was the perfect embodiment of manhood. He was totally secure in who He was, never once compromising His integrity, though faced with overwhelming circumstances. His life was completely authentic, and He shared it without reservation with the guys around Him. He courageously stood against the corrupt religious establishment and maintained self-control in the face of an unjust trial, beating, and execution. His loyalty to His Father allowed Him to patiently endure the Cross, where an incomprehensible paradox occurred. Both the love and wrath of God were poured out in full. The death and resurrection of Jesus bridged the gap created by our sin and made possible again a relationship with God, from whom all the great enthusiasm of life is derived. In short, He was and is the Ultimate Man.

The great mystery and fundamental truth of Christianity is that you can know Him. As you walk closely with Him, you will begin to notice something no amount of discipline will ever bring about: an inward transformation. Anyone can practice outward religion or morality and be a "good" person, but only Jesus can change one's heart. This heart change is absolutely necessary to become the man God made you to be. If you remember only one thing from this study, remember this: Be friends with Jesus. Know Him, study Him, share your life with Him, walk with Him, and most of all, love Him. Give Him your life and He will make you a man. As you live a life of obedience to Him, you take on His life. He lives through you. Do not forget that you are only a vessel. If we are great men or accomplish great things, it is only because the greatest Man is at work in us.

Never mistake practicing the disciplines given in this book for relationship with Jesus Himself. The disciplines are the means by which we walk closely with Him; Christ is the end. We have given you practical steps to take; you must decide to take them. We have shown you Christ; you must walk with Him.

NOTES

Checkpoint 1: Identity

1. C. S. Lewis, *The Complete C. S. Lewis Signature Classics: Mere Christianity* (New York: Harper Collins, 2007), 103.
2. Gary L. Thomas, *The Glorious Pursuit: Embracing the Virtues of Christ* (Colorado Springs, CO: NavPress, 1998), 35.
3. Review of John Maxwell, *Failing Forward* (Nashville: Thomas Nelson, 2000), http://julesyap.multiply.com/reviews/item/2?&show_interstitial= 1&u=%2Freviews%2Fitem, accessed February 9, 2012.
4. A. W. Tozer, *The Root of the Righteous* (Camp Hill, PA: Christian Publications, 1986), 137.

Checkpoint 2: Integrity

1. To learn more about Brandon Slay, visit www.brandonslay.com or www.greatergold.com.
2. "A New Generation Expresses Its Skepticism and Frustration with Christianity," The Barna Group (www.barna.org), September 24, 2007, http://www.barna.org/teens-next-gen-articles/94-a-new-generation-expresses -its-skepticism-and-frustration-with-christianity, used by permission.
3. Gary L. Thomas, *The Glorious Pursuit: Embracing the Virtues of Christ* (Colorado Springs, CO: NavPress, 1998), 35.

Checkpoint 3: Community

1. C. S. Lewis, *The Problem of Pain* (San Francisco: Harper, 1996), 125.
2. J. Oswald Sanders, *Spiritual Leadership: Principles of Excellence for Every Believer*, 2nd ed. (Chicago: Moody, 1994), 53.
3. C. S. Lewis, *The Four Loves* (London: Harcourt, 1988), 80.

Checkpoint 4: Self-Control

1. C. S. Lewis, *The Four Loves* (London: Harcourt, 1988), 8.
2. http://www.xxxchurch.com/whyporn/; "14 Shocking Pornography Statistics," *The United Families International Blog*, June 2, 2010,

http://unitedfamiliesinternational.wordpress.com/2010/06/02/14
-shocking-pornography-statistics/.

3. "Practical Outcomes Replace Biblical Principles As the Moral Standard,"
The Barna Group (www.barna.org), September 10, 2001, http://www
.barna.org/barna-update/article/5-barna-update/58-practical-outcomes
-replace-biblical-principles-as-the-moral-standard, used by permission.

4. Lewis, 115.

5. Dr. James Dobson, "Teen-ager's Discovery has Parent Hunting for Right
Words," Focus on the Family, February 24, 2002, http://www.uexpress
.com/focusonthefamily/index.html?uc_full_date=20020224.

6. "Facts on American Teens' Sexual and Reproductive Health," Guttmacher
Institute, December 2011, http://www.guttmacher.org/pubs/FB-ATSRH
.html.

7. Dietrich Bonhoeffer, *Creation and Fall & Temptation: Two Biblical Studies*
(New York: Touchstone, 1997), 132.

Checkpoint 5: Courage

1. Bill Tancer, *Click: What Millions of People Are Doing Online and Why It
Matters* (New York: Hyperion, 2008), 106.

2. Miroslav Volf, *Free of Charge: Giving and Forgiving in a Culture Stripped
of Grace* (Grand Rapids, MI: Zondervan, 2005), 209.

3. G. K. Chesterton, "The Exception Proves the Rule," in *The Collected
Works of G. K. Chesterton* (San Francisco: Ignatius Press, 1990), 111.

4. From the *Humanist Manifesto II*, 1973.

5. "Most Twentysomethings Put Christianity on the Shelf Following
Spiritually Active Teen Years," The Barna Group (www.barna.org),
September 11, 2006, http://www.barna.org/barna-update/article/
16-teensnext-gen/147-most-twentysomethings-put-christianity-on-the
-shelf-following-spiritually-active-teen-years, used by permission.

6. Stu Weber, *Tender Warrior: Every Man's Purpose, Every Woman's Dream,
Every Child's Hope* (Sisters, OR: Multnomah, 1993), 41.

7. John Piper, *Don't Waste Your Life* (Wheaton: Crossway, 2003), 10.

8. Weber, 49.

Checkpoint 6: Patience

1. Some translations say "when you are angry" or "if you are angry,"
suggesting that we have options regarding righteous anger. The accurate
translation is "Be angry and do not sin." Don't mistake the command as a

license to be angry all the time; the verse is commanding anger when circumstances necessitate it. If a situation calls for anger and we do not respond with righteous indignation, we sin by our passivity—by the fact that we did *not* get angry (Daniel B. Wallace, *ExSyn*, 491–492; Wallace, "Ephesians 4:29," 367–368).

2. C. S. Lewis, "The Trouble with X," in *God in the Dock: Essays on Theology and Ethics*, ed. Walter Hooper (Grand Rapids, MI: Eerdmans, 2001), 154.

3. C. S. Lewis, *The Weight of Glory* (San Francisco: Harper, 1980), 26.

4. C. S. Lewis, "Answers to Questions on Christianity," in *God in the Dock: Essays on Theology and Ethics*, ed. Walter Hooper (Grand Rapids, MI: Eerdmans, 2001), 54.

5. C. S. Lewis, *Mere Christianity* (San Francisco: Harper, 1980), 136–137.

Checkpoint 7: Loyalty

1. George Barna, *Growing True Disciples: New Strategies for Producing Genuine Followers of Christ* (Colorado Springs, CO: Waterbrook, 2001), 34–35.

2. Barna, 44.

3. J. Oswald Sanders, *Spiritual Leadership: Principles of Excellence for Every Believer*, 2nd ed. (Chicago: Moody, 1994), 52.

4. Christina Rossetti, "Who Shall Deliver Me?" *The Complete Poems* (London: Penguin Books, 2001), 221.

Checkpoint 8: Enthusiasm

1. Gary L. McIntosh and Samuel D. Rima Sr., *Overcoming the Dark Side of Leadership: The Paradox of Personal Dysfunction* (Grand Rapids, MI: Baker, 2004), 43.

2. McIntosh and Rima, 180.

3. McIntosh and Rima, 191.

4. "Facts for Families: Teen Suicide," *American Academy of Child and Adolescent Psychiatry*, May 2008, http://aacap.org/page.ww?name=Teen +Suicide&section=Facts+for+Families.

5. "Teen Depression Statistics," *Tandem Journey*, http://www.tandemjourney .org/Page.asp?NavID=19.

6. "Teen Suicide Awareness: Statistics," *TeacherVision*, http://www .teachervision.fen.com/education-and-social-issues/mental-health/57131 .html#ixzz1XTS0oxTb.

7. McIntosh and Rima, 207.

8. A slight variation of a quote attributed to John Wesley.

Closing

1. C. S. Lewis, "Answers to Questions on Christianity," in *God in the Dock: Essays on Theology and Ethics*, ed. Walter Hooper (Grand Rapids, MI: Eerdmans, 2001), 50.

ABOUT THE AUTHORS

BRIAN MILLS has been in student ministry full-time since 2001. After graduating from Ouachita Baptist University, he has served in student ministries as small as seven and as large as three thousand. He is currently the youth pastor at Long Hollow Baptist Church in Hendersonville, Tennessee, where he oversees a student ministry that weekly reaches more than 1,500 students spread across four campuses. Brian is passionate about seeing students saved, baptized, and growing in their faith and enjoys leading his staff and volunteers.

Brian is the cofounder of the website www.reallifestudentministries .com with Jeff and Rachel Lovingood and has served on the board of Metro Youth Pastors (sixty of the largest SBC student ministries in the United States). He authored a five-part sermon series for *Josiah Road* and travels and speaks at DNOWs, camps, evangelistic events, and youth conferences in the United States.

Brian loves to hang with his family, play sports, golf, and spend time investing into the next generation. He is the father of two children, McKenna and Parker, and the husband of Jennifer Mills.

NATHAN WAGNON (ThM, Dallas Seminary) has been actively involved in generational discipleship and leadership training for more than a decade. He is an active-duty infantry officer assigned to the 4th Infantry Division at Fort Carson, Colorado. He and his wife, Margaret, serve at Woodmen Valley Chapel in Colorado Springs, Colorado.